INFANCY AND HISTORY

RADICAL THINKERS }V

SET 1 ($12/£6/$14CAN)

MINIMA MORALIA
Reflections on a Damaged Life
THEODOR ADORNO
ISBN-13: 978 1 84467 051 2

FOR MARX
LOUIS ALTHUSSER
ISBN-13: 978 1 84467 052 9

THE SYSTEM OF OBJECTS
JEAN BAUDRILLARD
ISBN-13: 978 1 84467 053 6

LIBERALISM AND DEMOCRACY
NORBERTO BOBBIO
ISBN-13: 978 1 84467 062 8

THE POLITICS OF FRIENDSHIP
JACQUES DERRIDA
ISBN-13: 978 1 84467 054 3

THE FUNCTION OF CRITICISM
TERRY EAGLETON
ISBN-13: 978 1 84467 055 0

SIGNS TAKEN FOR WONDERS
On the Sociology of Literary Forms
FRANCO MORETTI
ISBN-13: 978 1 84467 056 7

THE RETURN OF THE POLITICAL
CHANTAL MOUFFE
ISBN-13: 978 1 84467 057 4

SEXUALITY IN THE FIELD OF VISION
JACQUELINE ROSE
ISBN-13: 978 1 84467 058 1

THE INFORMATION BOMB
PAUL VIRILIO
ISBN-13: 978 1 84467 059 8

CULTURE AND MATERIALISM
RAYMOND WILLIAMS
ISBN-13: 978 1 84467 060 4

THE METASTASES OF ENJOYMENT
On Women and Causality
SLAVOJ ŽIŽEK
ISBN-13: 978 1 84467 061 1

SET 2 ($12.95/£6.99/$17CAN)

AESTHETICS AND POLITICS
THEODOR ADORNO, WALTER BENJAMIN, ERNST BLOCH, BERTOLT BRECHT, GEORG LUKÁCS
ISBN-13: 978 1 84467 570 8

INFANCY AND HISTORY
On the Destruction of Experience
GIORGIO AGAMBEN
ISBN-13: 978 1 84467 571 5

POLITICS AND HISTORY
Montesquieu, Rousseau, Marx
LOUIS ALTHUSSER
ISBN-13: 978 1 84467 572 2

FRAGMENTS
JEAN BAUDRILLARD
ISBN-13: 978 1 84467 573 9

LOGICS OF DISINTEGRATION
Poststructuralist Thought and the Claims of Critical Theory
PETER DEWS
ISBN-13: 978 1 84467 574 6

LATE MARXISM
Adorno, Or, The Persistence of the Dialectic
FREDRIC JAMESON
ISBN-13: 978 1 84467 575 3

EMANCIPATION(S)
ERNESTO LACLAU
ISBN-13: 978 1 84467 576 0

THE POLITICAL DESCARTES
Reason, Ideology and the Bourgeois Project
ANTONIO NEGRI
ISBN-13: 978 1 84467 582 1

ON THE SHORES OF POLITICS
JACQUES RANCIÈRE
ISBN-13: 978 1 84467 577 7

STRATEGY OF DECEPTION
PAUL VIRILIO
ISBN-13: 978 1 84467 578 4

POLITICS OF MODERNISM
Against the New Conformists
RAYMOND WILLIAMS
ISBN-13: 978 1 84467 580 7

THE INDIVISIBLE REMAINDER
On Schelling and Related Matters
SLAVOJ ŽIŽEK
ISBN-13: 978 1 84467 581 4

INFANCY AND HISTORY
The Destruction of Experience

Giorgio Agamben

Translated by Liz Heron

VERSO

London • New York

First published as *Infanzia e storia* by Giulio Einaudi Editore in 1978
This edition first published by Verso 1993

© Giulio Einaudi 1978
Translation © Liz Heron 1993

This edition published by Verso 2007

Verso
UK: 6 Meard Street, London W1F 0EG
USA: 180 Varick Street, New York, NY 10014

Verso is the imprint of New Left Books

ISBN-13 978-184467-571-5

British Library Cataloguing in Publication Data
A catalogue record for this book is available from the British Library

Library of Congress Cataloging-in-Publication Data
A catalogue record for this book is available from the Library of Congress

Typeset by Hewer Text UK Ltd, Edinburgh
Printed and bound in Great Britain by Bookmarque Ltd, Croydon

Contents

Translator's Note

I have tried, wherever possible, to annotate quotations that had no references in the original, and to use published English translations of these quotations where they exist. I have found the French edition of *Infanzia e Storia* helpful in this respect. In other cases I have translated quotations directly from the French, and in instances where no English translation from the German is available, I have translated from the Italian, while consulting the French edition. I wish to thank Malcolm Imrie for the assistance he gave me in tracing references.

L.H.

PREFACE

Experimentum Linguae

Every written work can be regarded as the prologue (or rather, the broken cast) of a work never penned, and destined to remain so, because later works, which in turn will be the prologues or the moulds for other absent works, represent only sketches or death masks. The absent work, although it is unplaceable in any precise chronology, thereby constitutes the written works as *prolegomena* or *paralipomena* of a non-existent text; or, in a more general sense, as *parerga* which find their true meaning only in the context of an illegible *ergon*. To take Montaigne's fine image, these are the frieze of grotesques around an unpainted portrait, or, in the spirit of the pseudo-Platonic letter, the counterfeit of a book which cannot be written.

The best way of introducing this book, which will be read in English translation some fifteen years after the first Italian edition, would be to attempt to sketch the outlines of the unwritten work of which it forms the prologue, then possibly to refer to the later books which are its afterwords. In fact, between *Infancy and History* (1977) and *Il linguaggio e la morte*[1] (1982), many pages have been written which attest the project of a work that remains stubbornly unwritten. The title of this work is *La voce umana* (The Human Voice) or, as otherwise noted, *Etica, ovvero della voce* (Ethics, an essay on the voice). One of these pages contains this *incipit*:

Is there a human voice, a voice that is the voice of man as the chirp is the voice of the cricket or the bray is the voice of the donkey? And, if it exists, is this voice language? What is the relationship between voice and language, between *phōnē* and *logos*? And if such a thing as a human voice does not exist, in what sense can man still be defined as the living being which has language? The questions thus formulated mark off a philosophical interrogation. In the tradition of the ancients, the question of the voice was a cardinal philosophical question. *De vocis nemo magis quam philosophi tractant,* we read in Servius, and for the Stoics, who gave the decisive impulse to Western thinking on language, the voice was the *arkhē* of the dialectic. Yet philosophy has hardly ever posed the question of the voice as an issue . . .

It is significant that the author should have arrived at his inquiry into the human voice (or its absence) precisely through a reflection on infancy. In-fancy, which is this book's subject, is not a simple given whose chronological site might be isolated, nor is it like an age or a psychosomatic state which a psychology or a palaeoanthropology could construct as a human fact independent of language.

If every thought can be classified according to the way in which it articulates the question of the limits of language, the concept of infancy is then an attempt to think through these limits in a direction other than that of the vulgarly ineffable. The ineffable, the un-said, are in fact categories which belong exclusively to human language; far from indicating a limit of language, they express its invincible power of presupposition, the unsayable being precisely what language must presuppose in order to signify. The concept of infancy, on the contrary, is accessible only to a thought which has been purified, in the words of Benjamin writing to Buber, 'by eliminating the unsayable from language'. The singularity which language must signify is not something ineffable but something superlatively sayable: the *thing* of language.

This is why, in this book, infancy finds its logical place in a presentation of the relationship between language and experience.

Taking Benjamin's guidelines for his project of the philosophy to come, the experience at issue here can be defined only in terms of the 'transcendental experience' that was inadmissible for Kant.

One of the most urgent tasks for contemporary thought is, without doubt, to redefine the concept of the transcendental in terms of its relation with language. For if it is true that Kant was able to articulate his concept of the transcendental only by omitting the question of language, here 'transcendental' must instead indicate an experience which is undergone only within language, an *experimentum linguae* in the true meaning of the words, in which what is experienced is language itself. In his preface to the second edition of the *Critique of Pure Reason*, Kant presents as an *Experiment der reinen Vernunft* the attempt to consider objects in so far as they are 'only thought'. This, he writes, is an experience which is undergone not with objects, as in the natural sciences, but with concepts and principles which we admit *a priori* (such objects, he adds, 'must yet be able to be thought!').

In one of Erdmann's published fragments, this experiment is described as an 'isolation' of pure reason:

> I intend to examine how much reason can know *a priori* and to what extent it is independent of sensibility. . . . This question is a major and important one, since it shows man his destiny in relation to reason. To achieve such a goal, I deem it necessary to isolate reason [*die Vernunft zu isolieren*] as well as sensibility, considering only what can be known *a priori* and how it belongs in the realm of reason. This examination in isolation [*diese abgesonderte Betrachtung*], this pure philosophy [*reine Philosophie*] is of great usefulness.

One need only give close attention to the movement of Kantian thought to realize that the experiment in pure reason is necessarily an *experimentum linguae*, founded only on the possibility of naming the transcendental objects whereby Kant describes 'empty concepts without an object' (the *noumenon*, for example), which contemporary linguistics would call terms without a referent (but which retain, Kant writes, a transcendental *Bedeutung*).

Infancy is an *experimentum linguae* of this kind, in which the limits of language are to be found not outside language, in the direction of its referent, but in an experience of language as such, in its pure self-reference.

But what can an experience of this kind be? How can there be experience not of an object but of language itself? And, if so, without language experienced as this or that signifying proposition, but as the pure fact that one speaks, that language exists.

If for every author there exists a question which defines the *motivum* of his thought, then the precise scope of these questions coincides with the terrain towards which all my work is orientated. In both my written and unwritten books, I have stubbornly pursued only one train of thought: what is the meaning of 'there is language'; what is the meaning of 'I speak'? It is certainly clear that neither the speaking nor the being-spoken, which corresponds to it *a parte objecti*, is a real predicate which can be identified in this or that property (like that of being red, French, old, communist). They are, rather, *trascendentia* in the meaning of this term within medieval logic – that is, predicates which transcend all categories while insisting on each one of them; to be more exact, they have to be conceived as arch-transcendentals, or transcendentals to the second power, which, on Kant's scholastic list [*quodlidet ens est unum, verum, bonum seu perfectum*], transcend the very transcendentals and are implicated in each one of them.

To carry out the *experimentum linguae*, however, is to venture into a perfectly empty dimension (the *leerer Raum* of the Kantian concept-limit) in which one can encounter only the pure exteriority of language, that 'étalement du langage dans son être brut' of which Foucault speaks in one of his most philosophically dense writings. Every thinker has probably had to undertake this experience at least once; it is even possible that what we call thought is purely and simply this *experimentum*.

In his lectures on the *Essence of Language*, Heidegger talks about having an experience with language [*mit der Sprache eine Erfahrung machen*]. We have this experience, he writes, only where we lack names, where speech breaks on our lips. This breaking of speech is 'the backward step on the road of thought'. Whereas infancy is staked on the possibility that there is an experience of language which is not merely a silence or a deficiency of names, but one whose logic can be indicated, whose site and formula can be designated, at least up to a point.

In *Infancy and History*, the site of a transcendental experience of this kind lies in that difference between language and speech (Saussure's *langue* and *parole* – or rather, in Benveniste's terms, between semiotic and semantic) which cannot be encompassed, and which every reflection on language most confront. In showing that there is no way between these two dimensions, Benveniste led the science of language (and, with it, the entire cohort of the human sciences, with linguistics as their pilot science) face to face with the supreme aporia, beyond which it cannot advance without its transformation into philosophy. It is clear, therefore, that for a being whose experience of language was not always split into language and speech – in other words, a primordially speaking being, primordially within an undivided language – there would be no knowledge, no infancy, no history: he would already be directly one with his linguistic nature and would nowhere find any discontinuity or difference where any history or knowledge might be produced.

The double articulation of language and speech seems, therefore, to constitute the specific structure of human language. Only from this can be derived the true meaning of that opposition of *dynamis* and *energeia*, of potency and act, which Aristotle's thought has bequeathed to philosophy and Western science. Potency – or knowledge – is the specifically human faculty of connectedness as lack; and language, in its split between language and speech, structurally contains this connectedness, is nothing other than this connectedness. Man does not merely know nor merely speak; he is neither *Homo sapiens* nor *Homo loquens*, but *Homo sapiens loquendi*, and this entwinement constitutes the way in which the West has understood itself and laid the foundation for both its knowledge and its skills. The unprecedented violence of human power has its deepest roots in this structure of language. In this sense what is experienced in the *experimentum linguae* is not merely an impossibility of saying: rather, it is an impossibility of speaking *from the basis of a language*; it is an experience, via that infancy which dwells in the margin between language and discourse, of the very faculty or power of speech. Posing the question of the transcendental means, in the final analysis, asking what it means 'to have a faculty', and what is the grammar of the verb 'to be able'. And the only possible answer is an experience of language.

In my unwritten work on the voice, the site of this transcendental experience was sought instead in the difference between voice and language, between *phōnē* and *logos*, inasmuch as this difference opens the very space of ethics. From this perspective, there are numerous drafts transcribing the passage in the *Politics* where Aristotle, almost inadvertently, poses a decisive question which I set out to interpret:

> Nature, as we say, does nothing without some purpose; and for the purpose of making man a political animal she has endowed him alone among the animals with the power of reasoned speech. Speech is something different from voice, which is possessed by other animals also and used by them to express pain or pleasure; for the natural powers of some animals do indeed enable them both to feel pleasure and pain and to communicate these to each other. Speech on the other hand serves to indicate what is useful and what is harmful, and so also what is right and what is wrong. For the real difference between man and other animals is that humans alone have perception of good and evil, right and wrong, just and unjust. And it is the

sharing of a common view in these matters that makes a household [*oikìa*] or a city [*polis*].[2]

It has perhaps not been sufficiently noted that when, in *De interpretatione*, Aristotle defines linguistic signification by referring from the voice to the *pathemata* of the soul and to things, he is not merely speaking of *phōnē,* but uses the expression *ta en te phōnē,* what is in the voice. What is it in the human voice that articulates the passage from the animal voice to the *logos*, from nature to *polis*? Aristotle's response is well known: the voice articulates *grammata*, letters. The ancient grammarians began their argument with this opposition of the confused voice (*phōnē synkechyméne*) of animals and the human voice, which is instead *énarthros*, articulated. But if we ask in what this 'articulation' of the human voice consists, we see that for them *phōnē énarthros* simply means *phōnē engrámmatos, vox quae scribi potest*, the voice that can be written – in short, always pre-existing as written.

Aristotle's ancient commentators had asked why the philosopher had introduced the *gramma* as the fourth 'hermeneut' alongside the other three (voice, *pathemata*, things) which explain the circle of linguistic signification. So they attributed the particular status of the *gramma* to the fact that, unlike the other three, it is not just a *sign*, but also an element [*stoicheion*] of the voice, *as* articulation. As both a sign and a constitutive element of the voice, the *gramma* thus comes to assume the paradoxical status of an index of itself [*index sui*]. In this way, the letter is what always pre-exists within the moat between *phōnē* and *logos*, the primordial structure of signification.

The book I did not write had quite a different hypothesis. The moat between voice and language (like that between language and discourse, potency and act) can open the space of ethics and the *polis* precisely because there is no *arthros*, no articulation between *phōnē* and *logos*. The voice has never been written into language, and the *gramma* (as Derrida fortuitously demonstrated) is but the very form of the presupposing of self and of potency. The space between voice and *logos* is an empty space, a limit in the Kantian sense. Only because man finds himself cast into language without the vehicle of a voice, and only because the *experimentum linguae* lures him, grammarless, into that void and that *aphonia*, do an *ethos* and a community of any kind become possible.

So the community that is born of the *experimentum linguae* cannot take the form of a presupposition, not even in the purely 'grammatical' form of a self-presupposition. The speaking and the spoken with which we measure ourselves in the *experimentum* are neither a voice nor a *gramma*; as arch-transcendentals, they are not even thinkable as a quiddity, a *quid* of which we could ever, in Plotinus' fine image, take *moirai*, any share. The first outcome of the *experimentum linguae*, therefore, is a radical revision of the very idea of Community. The only content of the *experimentum* is that *there is language*; we cannot represent this, by the dominant model in our culture, as *a* language, as a state or a patrimony of names and rules which each people transmit from generation to generation. It is, rather, the unpresupposable non-latency in which men have always dwelt, and in which, speaking, they move and breathe. For all the forty millennia of *Homo sapiens*, man has not yet ventured to assume this non-latency, to have the experience of his speaking being.

In the only public lecture he ever gave, before the members of a club self-styled 'the heretics', Wittgenstein reproposes his own *experimentum linguae*:

> 'And now I shall describe the experience of wonderment before the existence of the world, with these words: the world thus is experienced as a miracle. I am now tempted to say that the correct expression in language for the miracle of the existence of the world, albeit as expressing nothing *within* language, is the existence of language itself.'

Let us try to follow through Wittgenstein's experiment, by asking ourselves: if the most appropriate expression of wonderment at the existence of the world is the existence of language, what then is the correct expression for the existence of language?

The only possible answer to this question is: human life, as *ethos*, as ethical way. The search for a *polis* and an *oikìa* befitting this void and unpresupposable community is the *infantile* task of future generations.

Giorgio Agamben, 1988–9

NOTES

1. Giorgio Agamben, *Language and Death: The Place of Negativity*, transl. Karen E. Pinkens with Michael Hardt, Minneapolis: University of Minnesota Press 1991.
2. Aristotle, *The Politics*, transl. J. Sinclair, Harmondsworth: Penguin 1962, Book 1, ch. 2, pp. 28–9.

INFANCY AND HISTORY

An Essay on the Destruction of Experience

To Claudia Rugafiori
O matematici, fate lume a tale errore! Lo spirito non ha voce, perché dov'é voce è corpo.
[O mathematicians, shed light on error such as this! The spirit has no voice, because where there is voice there is body.]

LEONARDO DA VINCI

One

The question of experience can be approached nowadays only with an acknowledgement that it is no longer accessible to us. For just as modern man has been deprived of his biography, his experience has likewise been expropriated. Indeed, his incapacity to have and communicate experiences is perhaps one of the few self-certainties to which he can lay claim. As long ago as 1933 Benjamin had accurately diagnosed this 'poverty of experience' of the modern age; he located its origins in the catastrophe of the First World War, from whose battlefields:

> men returned . . . grown silent – not richer, but poorer in communicable experience . . . What ten years later was poured out in the flood of war books was anything but experience that goes from mouth to mouth. And there was nothing remarkable about that. For never has experience been contradicted more thoroughly than strategic experience by tactical warfare, economic experience by inflation, bodily experience by mechanical warfare, moral experience by those in power. A generation that had gone to school on a horse-drawn streetcar now stood under the open sky in a countryside in which nothing remained unchanged but the clouds, and beneath these clouds, in a field of force of destructive torrents and explosions, was the tiny, fragile human body.[1]

Today, however, we know that the destruction of experience no longer necessitates a catastrophe, and that humdrum daily life in any city will suffice. For modern man's average day contains virtually nothing that can still be translated into experience. Neither reading the newspaper, with its abundance of news that is irretrievably remote from his life, nor sitting for minutes on end at the wheel of his car in a traffic jam. Neither the journey through the nether world of the subway, nor the demonstration that suddenly blocks the street. Neither the cloud of tear gas slowly dispersing between the buildings of the city centre, nor the rapid blasts of gunfire from who knows where; nor queuing up at a business counter, nor visiting the Land of Cockayne at the supermarket, nor those eternal moments of dumb promiscuity among strangers in lifts and buses. Modern man makes his way home in the evening wearied by a jumble of events, but however entertaining or tedious, unusual or commonplace, harrowing or pleasurable they are, none of them will have become experience.

It is this non-translatability into experience that now makes everyday existence intolerable – as never before – rather than an alleged poor quality of life or its meaninglessness compared with the past (on the contrary, perhaps everyday existence has never been so replete with meaningful events). It is not until the nineteenth century that we find the first literary indications of this everyday oppressiveness, and certain well-known pages of *Sein und Zeit* on the 'banality' of the quotidian (in which European society between the wars was all too ready to recognize itself) would simply have made no sense even just a century earlier, but this is precisely because the everyday – not the unusual – made up the raw material of experience which each generation transmitted to the next. Hence the unreliability of travellers' tales and medieval bestiaries; in no sense 'fantastical', they merely demonstrate that the unusual could not in any way be translated into experience. Each event, however commonplace and insignificant, thus became the speck of impurity around which experience accrued its authority, like a pearl. For experience has its necessary correlation not in knowledge but in authority – that is to say, the power of words and narration; and no one now seems to wield sufficient authority to guarantee the truth of an experience, and if they do, it does not in the least occur to them that their own authority has its roots in an experience. On the contrary, it is the character of the present time that all authority is founded on what cannot be experienced, and nobody would be inclined to accept the validity of an authority whose sole claim to legitimation was experience. (The youth movements' denial of the merits of experience is eloquent proof of this.)

Hence the disappearance of the maxim and the proverb, which were the guise in which experience stood as authority. The slogan, which has replaced them, is the proverb of humankind to whom experience is lost. This does not mean that today there are no more experiences, but they are enacted outside the individual. And it is interesting that the individual merely observes them, with relief. From this point of view a visit to a museum or a place of touristic pilgrimage is particularly instructive. Standing face to face with one of the great wonders of the world (let us say the *patio de los leones* in the Alhambra), the overwhelming majority of people have no wish to experience it, preferring instead that the camera should. Of course the point is not to deplore this state of affairs, but to take note of it. For perhaps at the heart of this apparently senseless denial there lurks a grain of wisdom, in which we can glimpse the germinating seed of future experience. The task which this essay proposes, taking up the legacy of Benjamin's project 'of the coming philosophy',[2] is to prepare the likely ground in which this seed can mature.

GLOSS

A story by Tieck, titled *Das Lebensüberfluss* (Life's Superfluity), depicts two penniless lovers who gradually renounce all possessions and all outside life to the point where they live closed up in their room. Finally, when they can no longer find wood for fuel, they burn the wooden ladder connecting their room with the rest of the house, and are left in isolation from the outside world, owning nothing and alive to nothing but their love. This ladder – Tieck gives us to understand – is experience, sacrificed by them to the flames of 'pure knowledge'. When the owner of the house (who here represents the claims of experience) returns and looks for the old ladder that led to the floor rented by the two young tenants, Heinrich (as the male protagonist is called) derides him with these words:

'He wishes that old experience should support him, like a man on the ground who would raise himself up, one step at a time, to the heights of highest understanding; but never thus will he be able to attain the immediate intuition of those who, like us, have now abolished all those trivial moments of experience and its stages, to sacrifice them, as the ancient Parsee law so has it, to the living, purifying flame of pure knowledge.'

Tieck explains the elimination of the ladder – i.e. experience – as a 'philosophy of poverty imposed on them by fate'. It is just such a 'philosophy of poverty' that can explain the modern rejection of experience by the young (but not only the young: 'metropolitan Indians' and tourists, hippies and family breadwinners alike are affiliated – far more than they would be prepared to acknowledge – by the same expropriation of experience). For they are like those cartoon characters of our childhood who can walk on thin air as long as they don't notice it; once they realize, once they experience this, they are bound to fall.

For this reason, even if objectively their condition is a dreadful one, there has never been a more revolting sight than that of a generation of adults which, having destroyed all remaining possibilities of authentic experience, lays its own impoverishment at the door of a younger generation bereft of the capacity for experience. When humankind is deprived of effective experience and becomes subjected to the imposition of a form of experience as controlled and manipulated as a laboratory maze for rats – in other words, when the only possible experience is horror or lies – then the rejection of experience can provisionally embody a legitimate defence.

The widespread existence of drug addiction today can also be seen in terms of this destruction of experience. What distinguishes modern addicts from the intellectuals who discovered drugs in the nineteenth century is that the latter (at least the less lucid among them) could still delude themselves that they were undergoing a new experience, while for the former this is nothing more than the discarding of all experience.

Two

In one sense, the expropriation of experience was implicit in the founding project of modern science.

> There remains but mere experience, which when it offers itself is called chance; when it is sought after, experiment. But this kind of experience is nothing but a loose faggot, and mere groping in the dark, as men at night try all means of discovering the right road, whilst it would be better and more prudent either to wait for day or procure a light and then proceed. On the contrary the real order of experience begins by setting up a light, and then shows the road by it, commencing with a regulated and digested, not a misplaced and vague course of experiment, and thence deducing axioms, and from these axioms new experiments . . .[1]

In these words of Francis Bacon, experience in the traditional sense – meaning what can be translated into maxims and proverbs – is already condemned irretrievably. The distinction between logical truths and truths of sufficient reason (which Leibniz formulates thus: 'When we expect the sun to rise tomorrow we are acting as empiricists because it has always been so until today. The astronomer alone can judge with sufficient reason') subsequently sanctions this condemnation. Because, against repeated claims to the contrary, modern science has its origins in an unprecedented mistrust of experience as it was traditionally understood (Bacon defines it as a 'forest' and a 'maze' which has to be put in order).

The view through Galileo's telescope produced not certainty and faith in experience but Descartes's doubt, and his famous hypothesis of a demon whose only occupation is to deceive our senses.

The scientific verification of experience which is enacted in the experiment – permitting sensory impressions to be deduced with the exactitude of quantitative determinations and, therefore, the prediction of future impressions – responds to this loss of certainty by displacing experience as far as possible outside the individual: on to instruments and numbers. But traditional experience thereby lost all real value. For – as demonstrated by the last work of European culture still integrally based on experience: Montaigne's *Essays* – experience is incompatible with certainty, and once an experience has become measurable and certain, it immediately loses its authority. There is no formulating a maxim nor telling a story where scientific law holds sway. Experience, with which Montaigne concerns himself, took so little account of science that he goes so far as to define its substance as a 'subject informe, qui ne peut rentrer en production ouvragère'[2] on which it is impossible to base any firm judgement ('il n'y a aucune constante existence, ny de notre estre, ny de celui des objects. . . . Ainsin il ne se peut establir rien de certain de l'un à l'autre . . .').[3]

The idea of experience as separate from knowledge has become so alien to us that we have forgotten that until the birth of modern science experience and science each had their own place. What is more, they were even connected to different subjects. The subject of experience was common sense, something existing in every individual (Aristotle's 'judging principle' and the *vis aestimativa* of medieval psychology, neither of them quite what we mean by good sense), while the subject of science is the *noūs* or the active intellect, which is separate from experience, 'impassive' and 'divine' (though, to be precise, knowledge did not even have a subject in the modern sense of an *ego*, but rather the single individual was the *sub-jectum* in which the active, unique and separate intellect actuated knowledge).

It is in this separation between experience and science that we have to see the meaning – an extremely concrete one, in no way abstruse – of the disputes dividing Aristotelian interpreters in late Antiquity and the Middle Ages on the singularity and separation of the intellect and its communication with the subjects of experience. Mind [*noûs*] and soul [*psychê*] are not one and the same thing for ancient thought (nor for medieval thought, at least up to Aquinas), and the intellect is not, as we are accustomed to think, a 'faculty' of the soul: it does not belong to it in any way, but is 'separate, individuated, impassive', according to the celebrated Aristotelian formula, and communicates with it to bring about knowledge. Consequently, for Antiquity, the central problem of knowledge is not the relationship between a subject and an object, but the relationship between the one and the many. Thus classical thought takes no cognizance of the question of experience as such, but what is posed for us as the question of experience arose naturally in Antiquity as the question of the relation (of the 'participation', but also of the 'difference', as Plato will say) between the separate intellect and particular individuals, between the one and the many, between the intelligible and the sensory, between the human and the divine. It is this difference which the chorus in Aeschylus' *Oresteia* underlines, characterizing human knowledge – against Agamemnon's *hubris* – as a *páthei máthos*, what is learned only through and after suffering, and excludes any possibility of foresight – that is, of knowing anything whatsoever with certainty.

Traditional experience (in the sense with which Montaigne is concerned) remains faithful to this separation of experience and science, human knowledge and divine knowledge. It is in fact the experience of the boundary between these two spheres. This boundary is death. Hence Montaigne can formulate the ultimate goal of experience as a nearing to death – that is, man's advance to maturity through an anticipation of death as the extreme limit of experience. But for Montaigne this limit remains something that cannot be experienced, which can only be approached ('si nous ne pouvons le joindre, nous le pouvons approcher'). But at the very moment when he is urging us to become 'familiar' with death and to 'cast off its strangeness' ('ostons luy l'estrangeté, pratiquons le, n'ayon rien si souvent en teste que la mort') he reverts to irony about those philosophers 'si excellens mesnagers du temps, qu'ils ont essayé en la mort mesme de la gouster et savourer, et ont bandé leur esprit pour voir que c'estoit ce passage; mais il ne sont pas revenus nous en dire les nouvelles'.[4]

In its search for certainty, modern science abolishes this separation and makes experience the locus – the 'method'; that is, the pathway – of knowledge. But to do this it must begin to recast experience and rethink intelligence, first of all expropriating their different subjects and replacing them with a single new subject. For the great revolution in modern science was less a matter of opposing experience to authority (the *argumentum ex re* against the *argumentum ex verbo*, which are not in fact irreconcilable) than of referring knowledge and experience to a single subject, which is none other than their conjunction at an abstract Archimedian point: the Cartesian *cogito*, consciousness.

Through this interpolation of experience and science in a single subject (which, being universal and bounded and at the same time an *ego*, unites in itself the properties of the separate intellect and the subject of experience), modern science re-effects that liberation from the *páthei máthos* and that conjunction of human knowledge with divine knowledge which constituted the precise character of the experience of the Mysteries and found their pre-scientific expression in astrology, alchemy and Neoplatonic speculation. For it was not in classical philosophy but in the sphere of the religious mysteries of late Antiquity that the boundary between the human and the divine, between the *pátheimáthos* and pure science (which, according to Montaigne, can only be approached, never touched) was crossed for the first time, in the idea of unutterable *páthēma* in which the initiate experienced his own death ('he knows the end of life', says Pindar) and thereby acquired the means 'to see a sweeter prospect of death and time gone by'.

The Aristotelian conception of homocentric celestial spheres as pure, divine, 'intelligences', immune from change and corruption and separate from the earthly sublunar world which is the site of change and corruption, rediscovers its original sense only if it is placed in the context of a culture which conceives of experience and knowledge as two autonomous spheres. Connecting the 'heavens' of a pure intelligence with the 'earth' of individual experience is the great discovery of astrology, making it not an antagonist, but a necessary condition of modern science. Only because astrology (like alchemy, with which it is allied) had conjoined heaven and earth, the divine and the human, in a single subject of fate (in the work of Creation) was science able to unify within a new ego both science and experience, which hitherto had designated two distinct subjects. It is only because Neoplatonic Hermetic mysticism had bridged the Aristotelian separation between *noŭs* and *psychē* and the Platonic difference between the one and the many, with an emanationist system in which a continuous hierarchy of intelligences, angels, demons and souls (think of the angel-intelligences of Avicenna and Dante) communicated in a 'Great Chain' which begins and ends with the One, was it possible to establish a single subject as the basis for 'experimental science'. It was by no means irrelevant that the universal mediator of this ineffable union between mind and senses, between the corporeal and incorporeal, the divine and the human, was, in the speculative thought of late Antiquity and the Middle Ages, a *pneuma*, a 'spirit', since it is precisely this 'subtle spirit' (the *spiritus phantasticus* of medieval mysticism) which will provide something more than a name for the new subject of science, which in Descartes is indeed manifest as *esprit*. The whole development of modern philosophy is contained, like a chapter in what Spitzer called 'historical semantics', by the semantic contiguity between *pneuma-spiritus-esprit-Geist*, and it is precisely because the modern subject of experience and knowledge – like the very concept of experience – has its roots in a mystical notion that any explication of the relationship between experience and knowledge in modern culture is bound to come up against almost insurmountable difficulties.

Through science, it is in fact Neoplatonic mysticism and astrology that make their entry into modern culture, not Aristotle's separate mind and incorruptible cosmos. And if astrology was subsequently abandoned (only subsequently: we must not forget that Tycho Brahe, Kepler and Copernicus were also astrologers, as was Roger Bacon, a fervent advocate of astrology who anticipates experimental science in many respects), it is because its fundamental principle – the union of experience and knowledge – had been so much assimilated as a principle of the new science through the constitution of a new subject that its essentially mythic-divine apparatus became superfluous. The rationalism/irrationalism which is so irreducably a part of our culture has a hidden genesis in this primary kinship between astrology, mysticism and science; the astrological revival among Renaissance intellectuals is the most striking symptom of this. Historically, this genesis is linked to what has now been firmly established thanks to Warburghian philology: that the humanistic restoration of Antiquity was a restoration not of classical Antiquity but of the culture of late Antiquity, in particular of Neoplatonism and Hermeticism. Thus a critique of mysticism, astrology and alchemy must necessarily imply a critique of science, and only the recovery of a dimension in which science and experience were each to find their own place of origin could prevail over the rationalism/irrationalism opposition.

In the Mysteries, the conjunction of experience and knowledge consisted of an event without speech, which culminated in the death and rebirth of the silenced initiate. In alchemy, it was enacted in the process of Creation whose fulfillment it was. But in the new subject of science, it becomes something no longer unutterable, but something that is already spoken in every thought and every utterance; not a *páthēma*, but a *máthēma* in the original sense of the word: something that is always prescient in every act of knowledge, the basis and subject of every thought.

We are so used to representing the subject as a substantial

psychic reality – that is, as a consciousness perceived as the site of psychic processes – that we forget how, on its first appearance, the 'psychic' and substantial character of the new subject was certainly not obvious. At the moment of its manifest emergence in the Cartesian formulation, it is not in fact a psychic reality (it is neither Aristotle's *psychē* nor the *anima* of the medieval tradition), but a pure Archimedean point ('nihil nisi punctum petebat Archimeds, quod esset firmum ac immobile . . .')[5] which came into being precisely through the quasi-mystical reduction of all psychic content except the pure act of thought.

('Quid vero ex iis quae animae tribuebam? Nutriri vel incedere? Quandoquidem jam corpus non habeo, haec quoque nihil sunt nisi figmenta. Sentire? Nempe etiam hoc non fit sine corpore, et permulta sentire visus sum in somnis quae deinde animadverti me non sensisse. Cogitare? Hic invenio: cogitatio est; haec sola a me divelli nequit.')[6]

In its original pure state, the Cartesian subject is nothing more than the subject of the verb, a purely linguistic-functional entity, very similar to the 'scintilla synderesis' and the 'apex of mind' of medieval mysticism, whose existence and duration coincide with the moment of its enunciation.

('. . . hoc pronuntiatum, Ego sum, ego existo, quoties a me profertur, vel mente concepitur, necessario esse verum . . . Ego sum, ego existo; certum est. Quandiu autem? Nempe quandiu cogito; nam forte etiam fieri posset, si cessarem ab omni cogitatione, ut illico totus esse desinerem.')[7]

The impalpability and insubstantiality of this ego is betrayed by the difficulty Descartes experiences in naming it and identifying it outside the realm of the pure utterance *I think, therefore I am*, and the dissatisfaction with which, compelled to abandon the imprecision of the word *res*, he lists the traditional vocabulary of psychology ('res cogitans, id est mens, sive animus, sive intellectus, sive ratio'),[8] pausing at the end, with some hesitation, on the word *mens* (which, in the 1647 French edition of the *Meditations*, becomes *esprit*). None the less, immediately after (with a leap of logic whose incoherence did not escape the first readers of the *Meditations*, notably Mersenne and Hobbes, who reproaches Descartes over a deduction analogous to 'je suis promenant, donc je suis une promenade'), this subject is presented as a substance to which, as distinct from material substance, are attributed all the properties which characterize the soul of traditional psychology, including sensation ('Res cogitans? Quid est hoc? Nempe dubitans, intelligens, affirmans, negans, volens, nolens, imaginans quoque, et sentiens').[9] And it is this substantive I, in which the union of *noūs* and *psychē*, experience and knowledge, takes place, that provides the basis on which later thought, from Berkeley to Locke, will build the concept of a psychic consciousness replacing the soul of Christian psychology and the *noūs* of Greek metaphysics as a new metaphysical subject.

The transformation of its subject does not leave traditional experience unchanged. Inasmuch as its goal was to advance the individual towards maturity – that is, an anticipation of death as the idea of an achieved totality of experience – it was something complete in itself, something it was possible to have, not only to undergo. But once experience was referred instead to the subject of science, which cannot reach maturity but can only increase its own knowledge, it becomes something incomplete, an 'asymptotic' concept, as Kant will say, something it is possible only to *undergo*, never to *have*: nothing other, therefore, than the infinite process of knowledge.

Thus anyone proposing to recover traditional experience today would encounter a paradoxical situation. For they would have to begin first of all with a cessation of experience, a suspension of knowledge. But this is not to say that they would thereby have rediscovered the kind of experience which it is possible both to undergo and to have. The fact is that the old subject of experience no longer exists. It has split. In its place there are now two subjects, which are represented to us in a novel at the beginning of the seventeenth century (in the very same period when Kepler and Galileo are publishing their discoveries), advancing side by side, inseparable companions in a quest whose adventurousness matches its futility.

Don Quixote, the old subject of knowledge, has been befuddled by a spell and can only undergo experience without ever having it. By his side, Sancho Panza, the old subject of experience, can only have it, without ever undergoing it.

GLOSSES

I Fantasy and Experience

Nothing can convey the extent of the change that has taken place in the meaning of experience so much as the resulting reversal of the status of the imagination. For Antiquity, the imagination, which is now expunged from knowledge as 'unreal', was the supreme medium of knowledge. As the intermediary between the senses and the intellect, enabling, in phantasy, the union between the sensible form and the potential intellect, it occupies in ancient and medieval culture exactly the same role that our culture assigns to experience. Far from being something unreal, the *mundus imaginabilis* has its full reality between the *mundus sensibilis* and the *mundus intellegibilis*, and is, indeed, the condition of their communication – that is to say, of knowledge. And since, according to Antiquity, it is the imagination which forms dream images, this explains the particular relationship to truth which dreams have in the ancient world (like divination *per somnia*) and to efficacious knowledge (like medical treatment *per incubationem*). This is still true in primitive cultures. Devereux reports that the Mojave (not unlike other shamanistic cultures) believe that shamanistic powers and knowledge of myths, as well as the actions and chants that refer to them, are acquired in dreams – and, moreover, that if they were acquired in a waking state, they would remain sterile and ineffective until they were dreamed:

A shaman, who had allowed me to note down and learn his therapeutic ritual chant, explained that I would not have the same power to heal because I had not empowered and activated his chants through oneiric learning. Within the formula with which medieval Aristotelianism defines this mediating function of the imagination ('nihil potest homo intelligere sine phantasmate'),[10] the homology between phantasy and experience is still perfectly clear. But with Descartes and the birth of modern science, the function of phantasy is assumed by the new subject of knowledge: the *ego cogito* (observe that in the technical vocabulary of medieval philosophy, *cogitare* referred rather to the discourse of the imagination than to the act of intelligence). Between the new *ego* and the corporeal world, between *res cogitans* and *res extensa*, there is no need for any mediation. The resulting expropriation of the imagination is made evident in the new way of characterizing its nature: while in the past it was not a 'subjective' thing, but was rather the coincidence of subjective and objective, of internal and external, of the sensible and the intelligible, now it is its combinatory and hallucinatory character, to which Antiquity gave secondary importance, that is given primacy. From having been the subject of experience the phantasm becomes the subject of mental alienation, visions and magical phenomena – in other words, everything that is excluded by real experience.

II Cavalcanti and Sade (Need and Desire)

The removal of imagination from the realm of experience, however, casts a shadow on the latter. This shadow is desire, the idea of experience as fugitive and inexhaustible. For according to a notion already current in classical psychology and subsequently fully developed in medieval culture, imagination and desire are closely connected. Indeed, the phantasm, which is the true source of desire ('phantasia ea est, quae totum parit desiderium'), is also – as mediator between man and object – the condition for the attainability of the object of desire and therefore, ultimately, for desire's satisfaction. The medieval discovery of love in the works of the Provençal and *stilnovo* poets is, from this point of view, the discovery that love takes as its subject not the immediate sensory thing, but the phantasm; that is, simply the discovery of the phantasmatic character of love. But given the mediating nature of imagination, this means that the phantasm is also the subject, not just the object, of Eros. In fact, since love has its only site in imagination, desire never directly encounters the object in its corporeality (hence the apparent 'Platonism' of the erotic in *stilnovo* and troubadour poetry), but an image (an 'angel', in the strict sense of the word, for the love poets and the Arab philosophers: a pure imaging separate from the body, a *substantia separata* which, through its desire, moves the celestial spheres), a 'nova persona' which is literally the product of desire (Cavalcanti: 'Formando di desio nova persona'), within which the boundaries between subjective and objective, corporeal and incorporeal, desire and its object are abolished. It is precisely because here love is not the opposition between a desiring *subject* and an *object* of desire, but has in the phantasm, so to speak, its subject-object, that the poets can define its character (in contrast with a *fol amour* which can only consume its object without ever being truly united with it, without ever experiencing it) as a *fulfilled love* [*fin'amors*], whose delights never end ['gioi che mai non fina']. By linking this with Averroes's theory which sees in the phantasm the site of complete union between the individual and the active intellect, they can transform love into a soteriological experience.

But once imagination has instead been excluded from experience as unreal, and its place has been taken by the *ego cogito* (now the subject of desire, 'ens percipiens ac appetens', in Leibniz's words), the status of desire changes radically: it becomes essentially insatiable. At the same time the phantasm, which mediated and guaranteed the attainability of the object of desire (allowing it to be experienced), now becomes the very sum of its unattainability (its inexperiencibility). Thus in Sade (in contrast with Cavalcanti), the desiring I, excited by the phantasm ('il faut monter un peu son imagination', the Sadeian characters reiterate), finds before it only a body, an *objectum* which it can only consume and destroy without ever being satisfied, since in it the phantasm is infinitely elusive and hidden.

The expulsion of imagination from the sphere of experience indeed sunders what Eros – as the son of Poros and Penia – united in himself: *desire* (tied to imagination, insatiable and boundless) and *need* (tied to corporeal reality, measurable and theoretically able to be satisfied), in such a way that they can never coincide in the same subject. As the desiring subject, the Sadeian man always has before him another man as the subject of need, for need is nothing but the inverse form of his own desire and the sum of its essential otherness. It is this schism in Eros which Juliette expresses most acutely when, speaking of the special desire of the chevalier, who wants to satisfy himself with the *caput mortuum* of her digestion, she exclaims: 'Tenez, à l'instant, si vous le désirez; *vous en avez l'envie, moi j'en ai le besoin.*'

Hence the Sadeian universe's necessity of perversion, which, by conjoining need and desire, converts the essential frustration of desire into pleasure. For what the pervert recognizes is that it is his own desire (for what does not belong to him) that appears in the other as need. To Juliette's statement he could answer: 'What you feel as the intimate estrangement of corporeal need is what I feel as the estranged intimacy of desire: *your need is my want; my want is your need.*' If, in Sade – despite everything, and for all the expropriation of experience which he embodies so prophetically in the repetitive delirium of his characters – there is pleasure, there is joy; if in his novels there lives on a contorted version of the pure Edenic project of troubadour and *stilnovo* poetry, it is thanks to perversion, which, in the Sadeian Eros, fulfils the same function which *stilnovo* poetry entrusted to the phantasm and the woman-angel. Perversion is the redeeming archangel which rises in flight from the bloody theatre of Eros to raise the Sadeian man to heaven.

The split between need and desire, currently so much debated, is not something that can be healed voluntaristically, nor is it a knot that an ever blinder political practice can dissolve with a gesture. This should be eloquently evident from the place of desire in *Phenomenology of Spirit* (which Lacan, with customary acumen, was able to theorize as *objet à* and as *désir de l'Autre*). For in Hegel, desire – which emerges, significantly, as the first moment of self-consciousness – can only try to negate its own object, but never finds satisfaction in it. Indeed, the desiring I achieves a certainty of itself only through suppression of the other:

> Certain of the nothingness of this other, it explicitly affirms that this nothingness is *for it* the truth of the other; it destroys the independent object and thereby gives itself the certainty of itself. . . . In this satisfaction, however, experience makes it aware that the object has its own independence. Desire and the self-certainty obtained in its gratification are conditioned by the object, for self-certainty comes from superseding this other: in order that this supersession can take place, there must be this other. Thus self-consciousness, by its negative relation to the object, is unable to supersede it; it is really because of that relation that it produces the object again, and the desire as well.[11]

That pleasure which, in Sade, is made possible by perversion, in Hegel is enacted through the bondsman, who mediates the lord's pleasure:

> The lord relates himself mediately to the thing through the bondsman; the bondsman, *qua* self-consciousness in general, also relates himself negatively to the thing, and takes away its independence; but at the same time the thing is independent *vis-à-vis* the bondsman, whose negating of it, therefore, cannot go the length of being altogether done with it to the point of annihilation; in other words, he only works on it. For the lord, on the other hand, the immediate relation becomes through this mediation the sheer negation of the thing, or the enjoy-

ment of it. Desire fails to do this because of the thing's independence; but the lord, who has interposed the bondsman between it and himself, takes to himself only the dependent aspect of the thing and has the pure enjoyment of it. The aspect of its independence he leaves to the bondsman, who works on it.[12]

But the question which Sadeian man continues to ask amid the din of a dialectical machine which, *ad infinitum*, defers its answer to the total social process, is precisely this: 'What about the pleasure of the slave? And how can we once more join the two split halves of Eros?'

III Experience, Quest, Adventure

The problem of experience emerges in a specific way in the medieval *quests*. For the relationship between experience and science in the medieval Christian world is governed by a principle for which Honorius of Autun writes an exemplary formulation: 'Before original sin, man knew good and evil: good through experience [*per experientiam*], evil through science [*per scientiam*]. But, after sin, man knows evil through experience, and good only through science.' The quest – that is, the attempt of the man who can know good only *per scientiam* to experience it – expresses the impossibility of uniting science and experience in a single subject. Thus Percival, who *sees* the Grail but fails to experience it, is the emblematic figure of the quest – no less than Galahad, whose experience of the Grail is plunged into the ineffable. From this point of view, the Grail (the impossible vanishing point at which the break in knowledge is healed and the two parallel lines of science and experience meet) is simply what constitutes the matter of human experience as an aporia, literally as the absence of a road [*a-poria*]. Thus the quest is the direct opposite of that *scientia experimentalis* (though as such, it also prefigures it) whose project was already dreamt of by Roger Bacon at the end of the Middle Ages, and which will later find its codification with Francis Bacon.

While scientific experiment is indeed the construction of a sure road (of a *methodos*, a path) to knowledge, the *quest*, instead, is the recognition that the absence of a road (the *aporia*) is the only experience possible for man. But by the same token, the *quest* is also the opposite of the adventure, which in the modern age emerges as the final refuge of experience. For the adventure presupposes that there is a road to experience, and that this road goes by way of the extraordinary and the exotic (in opposition to the familiar and the commonplace). Instead, in the universe of the *quest* the exotic and the extraordinary are only the sum of the essential aporia of every experience. Thus Don Quixote, who lives the everyday and the familiar (the landscape of La Mancha and its inhabitants) as extraordinary, is the subject of a *quest* that is a perfect counterpart of the medieval ones.

IV The 'dark night' of Descartes

The affinity between mystical experience and the Cartesian experience of the *ego cogito* is more concrete than one might think. We have notes by Descartes such as the *Olympiques*, in which he describes how he had begun to understand the foundation for a marvellous discovery [*cepi intelliger fundamentum inventi mirabilis*]. According to Baillet, Descartes's first biographer, who transcribed these notes in the third person:

> On the tenth day of November one thousand six hundred and nineteen, having retired quite filled with his enthusiasm and entirely occupied by the thought of having on that day discovered the foundation of the marvellous science, he had three successive dreams in a single night, which he fancied could only have come from on high [there follows the account of the three dreams].

While he was still dreaming, Descartes began to interpret his own dream; on waking, he continued the interpretation 'calmly and . . . open-eyed':

The fright that had struck him in the second dream was, he believed, a mark of synderesis, that is to say a remorse of conscience for the sins which he must have committed throughout the course of his life until then. The thunderbolt that he heard was the sign of the Spirit of Truth which descended upon him to enter into him.[13]

Contrary to what Baillet appears to believe, synderesis is not a mere remorse of conscience; it is a technical term used in the Neoplatonic mysticism of the Middle Ages and the Renaissance to designate the highest and most delicate area of the soul; it is in direct communication with the supersensory, and has never been corrupted by original sin. Perhaps these pages give us a glimpse of the future experience of the *ego cogito*, and furnish one more proof of the close proximity between two poles of our culture which we tend all too often to perceive as antithetical. We see that the *cogito*, like mystical synderesis, is what remains of the soul when, at the end of a 'dark night', it is stripped of all its attributes and content. The heart of this transcendental experience of the I has been signally described by an Arab mystic, Al-Hallaj: 'I am *I* and the attributes are no more; I am *I* and the qualifications are no more . . . I am the pure subject of the verb.'

Three

It is in this context that we must place the Kantian formulation of the problem of experience. While identifying the content of possible experience with the science of his time – namely, Newtonian physics – Kant none the less poses the question of its subject with fresh rigour. Against the substantialization of the subject in a single psychic I, he begins by making a careful distinction between the *I think*, a transcendental subject which cannot be given substance or psychologized in any way, and psychological consciousness or the empirical I.

It is the old subject of experience which returns here to emerge autonomously as the empirical I, which is 'disjoined within itself and without relation to the identity of the subject', and, as such, lacks the capacity to be a basis for real knowledge. Beside it, as the condition for all knowledge, is the *I think*, transcendental consciousness – that is, the synthetical unitary source of consciousness, 'thanks to which only I can attribute to an identical me the multiplicity of my representations', and in the absence of which experience would never be knowledge, but only 'a rhapsody of perceptions'.

The coalescence of this duality in a single subject is explicitly refuted by Kant through, on the one hand, the discounting of intellectual intuition and, on the other, the critique of 'psychological paralogism' which is at the root of rational psychology. For Kant, since the transcendental subject cannot *know* an object (for this it needs the intuition furnished by sensory experience, being in itself incapable of intuition), but can only *think it*, it therefore cannot even know itself as a substantial reality which could be the object of a rational psychology:

We can, however, lay at the foundation of this science nothing but the simple and in itself perfectly contentless representation I, which cannot even be called a conception, but merely a consciousness which accompanies all conceptions. By this I, or He, or It, who or which thinks, nothing more is represented than a transcendental subject of thought = x, which is cognized only by means of the thoughts that are its predicates, and of which, apart from these, we cannot form the least conception. Hence we are obliged to go round this representation in a perpetual circle, inasmuch as we must always employ it, in order to frame any judgement respecting it. And this inconvenience we find it impossible to rid ourselves of, because consciousness in itself is not so much a representation governing a particular object, as a form of representation in general, insofar as it may be termed cognition; for in and by cognition alone do I think anything, . . . From all this it is evident that rational psychology has its origin in a mere misunderstanding. The unity of consciousness, which lies at the basis of the categories, is considered to be an intuition of the subject as an object; and the category of substance is applied to the intuition. But this unity is nothing more than the unity in *thought*, by which no object is given; to which therefore the category of substance – which always presupposes a given intuition – cannot be applied. Consequently, the subject cannot be cognized.[1]

Thus, the most rigorous formulation of the problem of experience concludes by positing it in terms of the inexperiencible. But the tenacity with which Kant defended the splitting of the I against all confusion and all loss of boundary shows how he saw the very condition for the possibility of knowledge precisely in this punctilious work of survey which marked off on all sides that transcendental dimension which 'is so named because it borders on the transcendent, and is thereby in danger of falling not only into the supersensory, but into that which is altogether senseless'.

The *Critique of Pure Reason* is the last place where the question of experience within Western metaphysics is accessible in its pure form – that is, without its contradictions being hidden. Original sin, with which post-Kantian thought begins, is the reunification of the transcendental subject and empirical consciousness in a single absolute subject.

In his *Encyclopaedia*, Hegel presents Kantian philosophy as having conceived of the spirit only as consciousness – that is, as opposed to self-consciousness and empirical consciousness – and therefore not arriving at 'the concept of the mind as in itself and for itself, thus as unifying consciousness and self-consciousness'. The idea of experience that flows from this unity can be grasped in the Introduction to *Phenomenology of Spirit* – which was originally titled *Science of the Experience of Consciousness*. For here experience ceases to be merely a means or a tool or a limit of consciousness, and becomes the very essence of the new absolute subject: its altering structure in the dialectical process.

> This *dialectical* movement which consciousness exercises on itself, and which affects both its knowledge and its object, is precisely what is called *experience [Erfahrung]*. . . . Consciousness knows *something*; this object is the essence or the *in-itself*; but it is also for consciousness the in-itself. This is where the ambiguity of this truth enters. We see that consciousness now has two objects: one is the first *in-itself*, the second is the *being-for-consciousness of this in-itself*. The latter appears at first sight to be merely the reflection of consciousness into itself, i.e. what consciousness has in mind is not an object, but only its knowledge of that object. But, as was shown previously, the first object, in being known, is altered for consciousness; it ceases to be the in-itself, and becomes something that is the *in-itself* only *for consciousness*. And this then is the True: the being-for-consciousness of this in-itself. Or, in other words, this is the *essence*, or the *object* of consciousness. This new object contains the nothingness of the first, it is what experience has made of it. . . . It shows up here like this: since what first appeared as the

object sinks for consciousness to the level of its way of knowing it, and since the in-itself becomes a *being-for-consciousness* of the in-itself, the latter is now the new object. Herewith a new pattern of consciousness comes on the scene as well, for which the essence is something different from what it was at the preceding stage. It is this fact that guides the entire series of the patterns of consciousness in their necessary sequence. . . . Because of this necessity, the way to Science is itself already *Science*, and hence, in virtue of its content, is the Science of the *experience of consciousness.*[2]

Heidegger rightly observes that in the phrase 'Science of the *experience of consciousness*' the genitive is subjective, not objective. 'Science of the *experience of consciousness*' means: consciousness, the new absolute subject, is in its essence a *path* towards science, an experience (*ex-*per-*ientia*, a 'coming-from and going-through') which is itself science. Thus experience here is simply the name for a basic characteristic of consciousness: its essential negativity, its always being what it has not yet become. Thus dialectic is not something that attaches itself to knowledge from outside: rather, it shows to what point in the new absolute subject (much further than in the Cartesian I) the essence of knowledge has now become identified with the essence of experience. The fact that consciousness has a dialectical structure means that it can never grasp itself as an entirety, but is whole only in the total process of its becoming, its 'calvary'. The negative character already implicit in traditional experience – in so far as this was always, as we have seen, an experience of death – becomes here the very structure of the human being.

Thus experience is now definitively something one can only undergo but never have. It is never accessible as a totality, it is never complete except in the infinite approximation of the total social process – like a 'foam of infinity', as in the image of the lines by Schiller which conclude *Phenomenology*, whereby Hegel defines the union of science and history in *Absolute Knowing.*

From the chalice of this realm of spirits
foams forth for him his own infinitude.[3]

The supremacy of the dialectic in our time, far beyond the limits of the Hegelian system, beginning with Engels's attempt to construct a dialectic of nature, has its roots in this conception of the negative and unattainable character of experience – that is, in an expropriation of experience which we are still largely living, and whose dialectic (as *dia-legesthai*, to concentrate and talk through) has precisely the role of conferring a semblance of unity. Thus, a critique of the dialectic is one of the most urgent tasks today for a Marxian exegesis truly freed from Hegelianism, if it is true – and it *is* true – that it is contradictory to proclaim the abolition of the Hegelian subject (consciousness) while retaining its essential structure and content through the dialectic.

It is on the overriding of the Kantian opposition between the transcendental and empirical I, and on the substantialization of the subject in a 'psyche', that nineteenth-century psychology constructs its central myth: that of a psycho-somatic I which is the incarnation of the mystical union between *noūs* and *psychē* on which ancient metaphysics had foundered. So-called scientific psychology, from Fechner to Weber and Wundt, tries to sidestep the impossibility of the subject (Kant's psychological paralogism) being substantivated by rational psychology, and of empirical psychology going beyond the bounds of psychology. It tries to reach the subject by constructing itself as a science of *conscious facts*, which derive from a parallelism between the psychic phenomenon and the concomitant physiological phenomenon (for example, between a psychic state and a cerebral state, or between a sensation and a stimulus). But it is precisely the hypothesis of psychophysiological parallelism which betrays the metaphysical derivation of scientific psychology (which Bergson rightly traced back to the Cartesian opposition of *res cogitans* and *res extensa* at work within man) and the impossibility of its apprehending the fact of consciousness, which it split in two, simultaneously as a physiological process and as consciousness. This possibility was, moreover, refuted by Leibniz with reference to the mechanical explanation of perception – that is, 'through figures and movements'. 'Supposing that there were a machine,' he writes in *Monadology.*

> 'whose structure produced thought, sensation, and perception, we could conceive of it as increased in size with the same proportions until one was able to enter into its interior, as he would into a mill. Now, on going into it he would find only pieces working upon one another, but never would he find anything to explain Perception.'[4]

This is the circle within which nineteenth-century psychophysiology remains imprisoned, and it is within this circle that modern psychiatry has found its space. Its basic paradox is apparent in the frankness with which Bleuler states, at the start of his *Textbook of Psychiatry*, that we cannot define consciousness except as 'the subjective element of a psychic process' – an element that can, however, be grasped directly 'only in its own interiority'.

It is on a critique of nineteenth-century psychophysiology that, at the end of the century, Dilthey and Bergson (and later Husserl and Scheler) base their attempt to gather 'life' into a 'pure experience'. Instead of the conscious facts which psychology sought to construct through their psychophysical substantialization, they posited the non-substantial and purely qualitative character of consciousness as revealed in immediate experience: the 'pure duration' of Bergson, the *Erlebnis* of Dilthey. The entire 'philosophy of life', as well as a good part of turn-of-the-century culture, including poetry, set out to capture this lived experience as introspectively revealed in its preconceptual immediacy. The inner sense which, for Kant, was without cognitive value and, with its 'rhapsody of perceptions', expressed only the impossibility of the transcendental I knowing itself, now became the source of the most authentic experience. But it is precisely in *Erlebnis*'s idea of 'lived experience' (as in the ideas of 'pure duration' and 'lived time'), that the philosophy of life betrays its contradictions.

In *Erlebnis*, inner experience is in fact revealed as a 'current of consciousness' which has neither beginning nor end and which, being purely qualitative, can be neither halted nor measured. Thus Dilthey compares our being as revealed in inner experience [*innere Erfahrung*] to a plant whose roots are buried in the earth and which only bears its leaves aloft, while Bergson's explanation of the act with which we accede to the flux of states of consciousness, and to duration in its purest sense, has recourse to *intuition*, which he can define only in the terms with which Neoplatonic mysticism characterized the union with the One: 'It is the direct vision of the mind by the mind . . . spontaneous consciousness, a vision barely distinct from the object which it sees.' Or by comparing it to the inspiration which suddenly places the writer 'au coeur même du sujet', and which is utterly elusive, because 'if one suddenly turns to grasp the impulse felt at one's back, it slips away.'[5]

So, in the end, the philosophy of life delegates to poetry (which takes up the legacy only with the benefit of inventory, or gets stuck in a one-way street) or to mysticism (which takes it over with enthusiasm in the *fin-de-siècle* theosophical revival) the task of comprehending *Erlebnis* – namely, that pure experience which is to be its foundation. It is not accidental that Dilthey should arrive at a consideration of lived experience only in so far as it ceases to be 'mute' and 'obscure' to become 'expression' in poetry and literature, thereby converting the 'philosophy of life' into hermeneutics. Bergson ends up in prophetic expectancy of a 'diffuse mystical intuition' and a 'vision of the beyond in an expanded scientific experience'.

It is against this background that we need to place Husserl's attempt to install a transcendental experience of the Cartesian I within the 'current of the *Erlebnises*'. But the contradiction he encounters head on can be grasped in an exemplary way in a passage from the second of the *Cartesian Meditations*. He questions empirical psychology's potential to provide a source for the experience of consciousness:

In advance, as though this were obviously correct, one mis-interprets conscious life as a complex of data of 'external' and (at best) 'internal sensuousness'; then one lets form-qualities take care of combining such data into wholes. To get rid of 'atomism', one adds the theory that the forms or configurations are founded on these data necessarily and the wholes are therefore prior in themselves to the parts. But, when descriptive theory of consciousness begins radically, it has before it no such data and wholes, except perhaps as prejudices. Its beginning is the pure – and, so to speak, still dumb – psychological experience, which now must be made to utter its own sense with no adulteration. The truly first utterance, however, is the Cartesian utterance of the ego cogito . . .[6]

With this concept of *mute* experience (in a passage from *Lectures on Internal Time Consciousness* he writes, with reference to the originating current of inner temporality and its relationship with the subject: 'for all this we have no names'), Husserl had got closest to the idea of pure experience – that is, something anterior both to subjectivity and to an alleged psychological reality. It is strange that he then should have identified it with its 'expression' in the *ego cogito*, thus from *mute* to *voiced*. Perhaps the fact that in this passage the transcendental subject is grasped at once as an expression, hence as something linguistic, is not accidental; it allows us to question both the Cartesian foundation of certainty in the *ego cogito* as *pronuntiatum*, and Dilthey's identification of the *Erlebnis* and its expression. A theory of experience truly intended to posit the problem of origin in a radical way would then have to start beyond this 'first expression' with experience as 'still mute so to speak' – that is, it would have to ask: does a mute experience exist, does an *infancy* [*in-fancy*] of experience exist? And, if it does, what is its relationship to language?

GLOSSES

I Montaigne's Fall and the Unconscious

In Chapter VI of the second book of the *Essays*, which, as the title
– *De L'Exercitation* – suggests, contains a short treatise on
experience, Montaigne refers to an incident to which he seems
to attach particular importance. One day, he relates, he was riding
not far from his house on a small, none too steady horse, when:

> . . . one of my young men (a strong sturdy fellow), mounted
> upon a young strong-headed horse, and that a desperate hard
> mouth, fresh, lusty and in breath, to shew his courage, and to out-
> goe his fellowes, fortuned with might and maine to set spurres
> unto him, and giving him the bridle, to come right into the path
> where I was, and as a Colossus with his weight riding over me and
> my nag, that were both very little, he overthrew us both, and
> made us fall with our heeles upward: so that the nag lay along
> astonied in one place, and I in a trance grovelling on the ground
> ten or twelve paces wide of him; my face all torne and bruised, my
> sword which I had in my hand a good way from me, my girdle
> broken, with no more motion or sense in me than a stocke.

In the description of the moments in which he gradually recovers
his senses, Montaigne displays incomparable mastery:

> And when I began to see, it was with so dim, so weake and so
> troubled a sight, that I could not discern anything of the light.
> . . . Touching the functions of the soule, they started up and
> came in the same progresse as those of the bodie. I perceived
> myself all bloudy; for my doublet was all sullied with the bloud
> I had cast. . . . Me thought my selfe had no other hold of me
> but of my lips ends. I closed mine eyes to help (as me seemed)
> to send it forth, and tooke a kinde of pleasure to linger and
> languishingly to let my selfe go from my selfe. It was an
> imagination swimming superficially in my minde, as weake

and as tender as all the rest: but in truth, not only exempted
from displeasure, but rather commixt with that pleasant sweet-
nesse which they feel that suffer themselves to fall into a soft-
slumbring and sense-entrancing sleepe.

This memory furnishes Montaigne with the pretext for a series of
digressions, where the twilight state comes to stand for a form of
experience which, albeit specific, is also in a sense experience at its
extreme and most authentic, emblematically summing up the
entire scope of inquiry of the *Essays*. Because his unconscious state
appears to him like the one 'they find themselves in, whom in the
agony of death we see to droop and faint thorow weaknesse: and
am of opinion we plaine and moane them without cause, esteem-
ing that either they are agitated with grievous pangs or that their
soule is pressed with painfull cogitations'. He adds: 'I have ever
thought they had their soule and body buried and asleepe: *vivit, et
est vitae nescius ipse suae.* And I could not believe that at so great an
astonishment of members and deffailance of senses the soule could
maintain any face within, to know herselfe.' Something very
similar takes place when we are drowsing, in the first 'stuttering'
of sleep, before it has completely overcome us, when we

. . . apprehend as it were in a slumber, what is done about us,
and with a troubled and uncertaine hearing, follow the voyces,
which seeme to sounde but on the outward limits of our soule;
and frame answers according to the last words we heard, which
taste more of chance than of sense. . . . My stomach was
surcharged with clotted bloud, my hands of themselves were
still running to it, as often they are wont (yea against the
knowledge of our will) when we feel it to itch. There are many
creatures, yea and some men, in whom after they are dead we
may see their muskles to close and stirre. All men know by
experience, there be some parts of our bodies which often
without any consent of ours doe stirre, stand, and lye down
againe. Now these passions, which but exteriorly touch us,

cannot properly be termed ours; for to make them ours, a man must wholly be engaged unto them: And the paines that our feet or hands feele whilst we sleepe are not ours.

There are, therefore, experiences which do not belong to us, which we cannot call 'ours', but which, for this very reason, precisely because they are experiences of the inexperiencible, constitute the extreme limit against which our experience can press, straining towards death. Montaigne concludes:

This discourse of so slight an accident is but vaine and frivolous were not the instructions I have drawne from thence for my use: for truly, for a man to acquainte himselfe with death, I find no better way than to approach unto it. . . . This is not my doctrine, it is but my study and not another man's lesson, but mine owne . . .[7]

Two centuries later, in the *Reveries of the Solitary Walker*, Rousseau refers to an episode so similar that, were we not to see in it all that weary sensuality we are accustomed to find in Jean-Jacques, we might think of a direct line of descent from Montaigne:

At about six in the evening I was on the hill leading down from Ménilmontant, almost opposite the Jolly Gardener, when some people walking in front of me suddenly stepped aside and I saw a Great Dane rushing at full tilt towards me, followed by a carriage. It saw me too late to be able to check its speed or change its course. I judged that my only hope of avoiding being knocked down was to leap into the air at precisely the right moment to allow the dog to pass underneath me. This lightning plan of action, which I had no time either to examine or to put into practice, was my last thought before I went down. I felt neither the impact nor my fall, nor indeed anything else until I eventually came to.

  It was nearly night when I regained consciousness. I was in the arms of two or three young men who told me what had happened. The Great Dane, unable to check its onrush, had run straight into my legs and its combined mass and speed had caused me to fall forward on my face. My upper jaw, bearing the full weight of my body, had struck against the extremely bumpy cobblestones, and my fall had been all the more violent because I was on a downhill slope, so that my head finished up lower than my feet. The carriage to which the dog belonged was directly behind it and would have run right over me had not the coachman instantly reined up his horses. So much I learned from those who had picked me up and were still holding me when I came to. But what I felt at that moment was too remarkable to be passed over in silence.

Night was coming on. I saw the sky, some stars, and a few leaves. This first sensation was a moment of delight. I was conscious of nothing else. In this instant I was being born again, and it seemed as if all I perceived was filled with my frail existence. Entirely taken up by the present, I could remember nothing; I had no distinct notion of myself as a person, nor had I the least idea of what had just happened to me. I did not know who I was, nor where I was; I felt neither pain, fear, nor anxiety. I watched my blood flowing as I might have watched a stream, without even thinking that the blood had anything to do with me. I felt throughout my whole being such a wonderful calm, that whenever I recall this feeling I can find nothing to compare with it in all the pleasures that stir our lives.[8]

Here, too, a twilight unconscious state becomes the matrix of a specific experience – not, however, an anticipation of death, as in Montaigne, but rather an experience of birth ('In this instant I was being born again') and simultaneously the key to an incomparable pleasure.

These episodes are two lone messengers heralding the surging emergence of the concept of the unconscious in the nineteenth century, from Schelling to Schopenhauer up to its original reformulation in the work of Freud. This concept is of interest to us here only for its implications for a theory of experience – that is, as a symptom of malaise. For the crisis of the modern concept of experience – experience founded on the Cartesian subject – is certainly at its most salient in the idea of the unconscious. As its attribution to a third person, an *Es*, clearly shows, unconscious experience is not a subjective experience, not an experience of the I. From the Kantian point of view, it cannot even be called an experience, for it lacks that synthetical unity of consciousness (self-consciousness) which is the fundament and the guarantee of every experience. None the less, psychoanalysis shows us indeed that the most important experiences are those that belong not to the subject, but to 'it' [*Es*]. The Id is not, however, deaf, as in Montaigne's fall; for now the limit of experience has been turned around: it is no longer deathwards, but backwards towards infancy. In this inversion of boundaries, as also in the passage from the first to the third person, we must decipher the features of a new experience.

II Modern Poetry and Experience

It is in the context of this crisis of experience that modern poetry finds its place. For, on close scrutiny, modern poetry from Baudelaire onwards is seen to be founded not on new experience, but on an unprecedented lack of experience. Hence the boldness with which Baudelaire can place shock at the centre of his artistic work. It is experience that best affords us protection from surprises, and the production of shock always implies a gap in experience. To experience something means divesting it of novelty, neutralizing its shock potential. Hence Baudelaire's fascination with commodities and *maquillage* – the supremely inexperiencible.

In Baudelaire, a man expropriated from experience exposes himself to the force of shock. Poetry responds to the expropriation of experience by converting this expropriation into a reason for surviving and making the inexperiencible its normal condition. In this perspective, the search for the 'new' does not appear as the search for a new object of experience; instead, it implies an eclipse and a suspension of experience. New is what cannot be experienced, because it lies 'in the depths of the unknown': the Kantian thing-in-itself, the inexperiencible as such. Thus, in Baudelaire (and this is the measure of his lucidity) this search takes the paradoxical form of aspiring to the creation of a 'lieu commun' – a common place ('créer un poncif c'est le génie' – to create a commonplace is genius; think of Baudelaireian poetic rhythms, with their sudden footholds in banality that so struck Proust). By this was meant what could be created only from a century's accumulation of experience, not invented by one individual. But in a state where man has been expropriated of experience, the creation of such a 'lieu commun' is possible only through a destruction of experience which, in the very moment of its counterfeit authority, suddenly discloses that this destruction is really man's new abode. Estrangement, which removes from the most commonplace objects their power to be experienced, thus becomes the exemplary procedure of a poetic project which aims to make of the Inexperiencible the new 'lieu commun', humanity's new experience. In this sense the *Fleurs du Mal* are proverbs of the inexperiencible.

But the most peremptory objection against the modern concept of experience has been raised in the work of Proust. For the object of the *Recherche* is not a lived experience but, quite the contrary, something which has been neither lived nor experienced. And not even its sudden emergence in the *intermittences du coeur* constitutes an experience, from the point when the condition of this emergence is precisely a vacillation of the Kantian conditions of experience: time and space. And it is not only the conditions of experience that are called into question, but also its subject, for the latter is undoubtedly not the modern subject of knowledge (Proust seems rather to have in mind certain crepuscular states, like drowsiness or a loss of consciousness: 'Je ne savais pas au premier instant qui j'étais' – I did not know who I was at first – is his typical formula, whose innumerable variations have been registered by Poulet). But we are not even dealing with the Bergsonian subject, to whose ultimate reality intuition gives us access. What intuition reveals is nothing other than the pure succession of states of consciousness, this still being something subjective; indeed, the subjective in its pure state, so to speak. Whereas in Proust there is no longer really any subject, but only – with singular materialism – an infinite drifting and a casual colliding of objects and sensations. Here the expropriated subject of experience emerges to validate what, from the point of view of science, can appear only as the most radical negation of experience: an experience with neither subject nor object, absolute. *L'inexpérience*, of which Proust died, according to Riviére ('. . . il est mort de ne pas savoir comment on allume un feu, comment on ouvre une fenêtre' – he died of not knowing how to light a fire or open a window), is understood in the literal sense: a refusal and negation of experience.

The awareness of an appalling expropriation of experience, of an unprecedented 'void of experience', is also at the heart of Rilke's poetry. But unlike Baudelaire and Rimbaud, who entrust humanity's new experience resolutely to the inexperiencible, he oscillates between two contradictory worlds. In the angel, the puppet, the acrobat and the child he holds up the figures of a *Dasein* which has totally freed itself from all experience; on the other hand, he evokes nostalgically the things in which individuals 'accumulated the human' (in the letter to Hulevicz, this process of 'accumulation' is identified with what makes things themselves experiencible) and which were thereby made 'liveable' [*erlebbaren*] and 'sayable' [*säglichen*], in contrast to the 'appearances of things' which 'bear down from America' and have now transposed their existence 'within the vibration of money'. The fact of being suspended between these two worlds like one of the 'disinherited' (each age, he writes in the seventh elegy, 'has such disinherited children, to whom no longer what's been, and not yet what's coming, belongs'[9]) is the central experience of Rilke's poetry, which, like many works deemed esoteric, has no mysticism in it, but concerns the daily life of a citizen of the twentieth century.

Four

Any rigorous formulation of the question of experience inevitably impacts on the question of language. This is where full weight must be given to Hamann's critique of Kant, which renders meaningless any idea of pure reason 'elevated as a transcendental subject' and asserted as independent of language; for 'not only does the faculty of thought wholly reside in language, but language is also reason's central misunderstanding of itself'. He rightly objected against Kant that the immanence of language for any and every act of thought, however a *priori*, would have made necessary a 'Metacritique of the purism of pure reason' – that is, a purging of language, something which could not, however, be posited in the terms of the *Critique*, since its problematic could be formulated only as a homology of reason and language: 'Reason is language: *lōgos*. This is the marrow bone at which I shall gnaw and gnaw until I die of it.'

It is Kant's situating of the problem of knowledge on the mathematical model that prevented him, as it did Husserl, from discerning the original place of transcendental subjectivity within language, and therefore from clearly tracing the boundaries separating the transcendental and the linguistic. This ommission ensures that in the *Critique* transcendental apperception emerges, almost naturally, as an 'I think', as a linguistic subject and even, in one extremely significant passage, as a 'text' (' "I think" is the sole text of rational psychology, from which it has to develop its entire science'). It is this 'textual' configuration of the transcendental sphere which, in the absence of a specific formulation of the question of language, situates the 'I think' in a zone where transcendental and linguistic seem to merge, and where Hamann could therefore justly validate the 'genealogical primacy' of language over pure reason.

It is significant that in one passage in the *Origin of Geometry*, where Husserl speculates about the ideal objectivity of geometric objects, he is led to pose the question of language as a condition of this objectivity:

> . . . how does geometrical ideality (just like that of all sciences) proceed from its primary intrapersonal origin, where it is a structure within the conscious space of the first inventor's soul, to its ideal objectivity? In advance we see that it occurs by means of language, through which it receives, so to speak, its linguistic living body [*Sprachleib*] . . .[1]

Only the persisting dominance of the geometric-mathematical model over the theory of knowledge can make any sense of the way in which Husserl – who even goes so far as to state that 'One is conscious of civilization from the start as an immediate and mediate linguistic community',[2] and that 'men as men, fellow men, world . . . and on the other hand, language, are inseparably intertwined; and one is always certain of their inseparable relational unity . . .'[3] – had avoided posing the question of the origins of language in relation to any possible transcendental perspective: 'Naturally, we shall not go into the general problem which also arises here of the origin of language . . .'.[4]

But if we take up Hamann's suggestion and abandon the clearcut model of transcendental mathematics – which has such ancient roots in Western metaphysics – to discover the fundamental and incontrovertible condition of any theory of knowledge in the elucidation of its relation to language, we then see that it is in language that the subject has its site and origin, and that only in and through language is it possible to shape transcendental apperception as an 'I think'.

Benveniste's studies on the 'Nature of Pronouns' and on 'Subjectivity in Language' – confirming Hamann's intuition of the necessity for a metacritique of the transcendental subject – show that it is in and through language that the individual is constituted as a subject. Subjectivity is nothing other than the speaker's capacity to posit him or herself as an *ego*, and cannot in any way be defined through some wordless sense of being oneself, nor by deferral to some ineffable psychic experience of the *ego*, but only through a linguistic I transcending any possible experience:

> However this subjectivity might be posited in phenomenology or psychology, it is but the emergence into being of a funda-mental property of language. He who says ego is 'ego'. It is here that we find the foundation of subjectivity, determined by means of the linguistic status of the person . . . such is the organization of language that it allows each speaker to appro-priate the entire language through the designation *I*.[5]

Only this exclusive instance of the subject in language can explain the specific character of the pronoun *I*, a stumbling block for Husserl, who had completely failed to grasp it, in so far as he believed he could account for it thus:

> In solitary discourse, the meaning [*Bedeutung*] of *I* has its essential realization in the immediate representation of our own personality, and that is also where the meaning of this word resides in the discourse of communication. Each interlocutor has his own representation of the I (and therefore his individual concept of the *I*); thus what is signified by this word changes with each individual.

But, here too, Benveniste shows that it is effectively impossible to have recourse to an 'immediate representation' and to an 'in-dividual concept' which individuals would have of themselves:

There is no concept *I* encompassing all the *I*s uttered at every single moment by every single speaker, in the sense that there is a concept 'tree' on which all individual uses of tree converge. There is no lexical entity named by the *I*. Can it then be said that the *I* refers to a particular individual? If that were so, it would be a permanent contradiction within language, and anarchy in practice: how could the same term relate indiscriminately to any given individual and at the same time identify the individual in his particularity? What we have before us is a class of words, 'personal pronouns', which elude the status of all other signs of language. To what does *I* then refer? To something very singular, which is exclusively linguistic: *I* refers to the act of individual discourse in which it is uttered, and it designates its speaker. It is a term that can only be identified within an instance of discourse. . . . The reality which it invokes is the reality of discourse.[6]

If this is true – if the subject has a 'reality of discourse' in the sense which we have seen, if this is nothing other than the shadow cast on man by the system of elocutionary indicators (which includes not only personal pronouns but all other terms which organize the subject's spatial and temporal relations: *this, that, here, now, yesterday, tomorrow*, etc.) – it then becomes clear to what extent the transcendental sphere as subjectivity, as an 'I think', is in fact founded on an exchange between the transcendental and the linguistic. *The transcendental subject is nothing other than the 'enunciator', and modern thought has been built on this undeclared assumption of the subject of language as the foundation of experience and knowledge.* And it is this exchange that has allowed post-Kantian psychology to confer psychological substance on transcendental consciousness – from the point when it emerged no less than empirical consciousness as an *I*, as a 'subject'.

Thus, if the rigorous Kantian distinction of the transcendental sphere must yet again be restated, it must, however, at the same time be flanked by a metacritique resolutely tracing the boundaries that separate it from the sphere of language and placing the transcendental beyond the 'text': *I think* – in other words, beyond the subject. The transcendental cannot be the subjective; unless transcendental simply signifies: linguistic.

Only on this basis does it become possible to pose the question of experience in unequivocal terms. For if the subject is merely the enunciator, contrary to what Husserl believed, we shall never attain in the subject the original status of experience: 'pure, and thereby still mute experience'. On the contrary, the constitution of the subject in and through language is precisely the expropriation of this 'wordless' experience; from the outset, it is always 'speech'. A primary experience, far from being subjective, could then only be what in human beings comes before the subject – that is, before language: a 'wordless' experience in the literal sense of the term, a human *infancy* [*in-fancy*], whose boundary would be marked by language.

A theory of experience could in this sense only be a theory of infancy, and its central question would have to be formulated thus: *is there such a thing as human in-fancy? How can in-fancy be humanly possible? And if it is possible, where is it sited?*

But it is easy to see that this in-fancy is not something to be sought, anterior to and independent of language, in a psychic reality of which language would be the expression. There are no subjective psychic facts, 'facts of consciousness', that a science of the psyche can presume to attain, independent of and outside the subject, for the simple reason that consciousness is solely the subject of language and cannot be defined except as – to quote Bleuler – 'the subjective attribute of psychic processes'. One can, of course, attempt to substantiate an in-fancy, a 'silence' of the subject, through the idea of a 'flux of consciousness', a primary psychic phenomenon that is fugitive and intangible; but once you aim to seize and concretize this primary current of the *Erlebnisse*, it proves possible only through the speech of the interior 'mono-logue', and Joyce's lucidity consists precisely in having understood that the flux of consciousness has no other reality than that of the 'monologue' – to be exact, that of language. Thus, in *Finnegans Wake*, the interior monologue can give way to a mythical absolutism of language beyond any 'lived experience' or any prior psychic reality. Of course one can make this human infancy correspond to Freud's unconscious, which occupies the submerged part of psychic territory; but as the Id, as a 'third person', it is in fact, as Benveniste shows yet again, a non-person, a non-subject (*al-ya'ibu*, the one who is absent, the Arab grammarians say), which has sense only in its opposition to the person. There is nothing untoward, then, when Lacan shows us that this Id also has no reality other than language, is itself language. (In passing, it should be said that the fact of having understood the instance of the Ego and the Id in language places the Lacanian interpretation of Freudianism decisively outside psychology.)

The idea of infancy as a pre-subjective 'psychic substance' is therefore shown to be as mythical as a pre-linguistic subject, with infancy and language seeming to refer back to one another in a circle in which infancy is the origin of language and language the origin of infancy. But perhaps it is in this very circle that we should seek the site of experience for human infancy. For the experience, the infancy at issue here, cannot merely be something which chronologically precedes language and which, at a certain point, ceases to exist in order to spill into speech. It is not a paradise which, at a certain moment, we leave for ever in order to speak; rather, it coexists in its origins with language – indeed, is itself constituted through the appropriation of it by language in each instance to produce the individual as subject.

If this is true, if we cannot reach infancy without encountering language – which seems to guard its gateway as the angel with the flaming sword guards the threshold of Eden – the question of experience as derivation of the human individual then becomes that of the origin of language in its double reality of *langue* and *parole*. Only by arriving at a point when the human individual existed, but language still did not, could we encompass this 'pure wordless experience'; an infancy both human and independent of language. But, from Humboldt on, linguistic science has demonstrated the fatuity of any such conception of the origin of language. 'We are always susceptible to a naive picturing of an original time when a complete man would have met his like, equally complete; gradually, between them, language would have been formed. That is pure fantasy. We never find man separated from language, and we never see him in the act of inventing it. . . . It is a speaking man that we find in the world, a man speaking to another man, and it is language whereby man is defined as man,' Humboldt wrote. It is through language, then, that the individual as known to us is constituted as an individual, and linguistics, however far back it goes in time, never arrives at a chronological beginning of language, an 'anterior' of language.

Does this mean that the human and the linguistic correspond exactly, and that the question of the origin of language should be set aside as extraneous to science? Or rather, that this problem is indeed the Impassable, in the face of which science finds its true place and its rigour? Must we really renounce the possibility of reaching this Impassable through the science of language; this infancy which alone would enable the foundation of a new concept of experience, freed from the subject's conditioning? In fact what we must renounce is merely a concept of origin cast in a mould already abandoned by the natural sciences themselves, one which locates it in a chronology, a primary cause which separates in time a before and after. Such a concept of origins is useless to the human sciences whenever what is at issue is not an 'object' presupposing the human already behind it, but is instead itself constitutive of the human. The origin of a 'being' of this kind cannot be *historicized*, because it is itself *historicizing*, and itself founds the possibility of there being any 'history'.

This is why every theory that sees language as a 'human invention' is always countered with one that sees it as a 'divine gift'. The clash of these two ideas and the progressive resolution of their opposition in the thought of Hamann, Herder and Humboldt marked the birth of modern linguistics. But the problem is not whether language is a *menschliche Erfindung* or a *gottliche Gabe*, for from the point of view of the human sciences both hypotheses border on myth; it is to realize that the origin of language must necessarily be located at a break with the continual opposition of diachronic and synchronic, historical and structural, in which it is possible to grasp as some kind of *Ur-event*, or *Urfaktum*, the unity – difference of invention and gift, human and non-human, speech and infancy. This is what Hamann does most categorically – albeit allegorically – when he defines human language as 'translation' from divine language, and thus identifies the origin of language and of knowledge in a *communicatio idiomatum* between human and divine.

Such a concept of origins is not in the least abstract, nor purely hypothetical; on the contrary, the science of language can produce concrete examples of it. For what is the Indo-European root, reinstated through philological comparison of the historical languages, if not an origin? An origin not merely pushed backwards in time, but equally representing a present, operative instance in the historical languages? It is located in a convergence of diachronic and synchronic, where, as a historically unattested state of the language – as 'never spoken language', yet still real – it guarantees both the intelligibility of linguistic history and the synchronic coherence of the system. An origin such as this can never be completely resolved through 'events' supposed historically to have occurred; it is something that has not yet ceased to occur. We can define this dimension as that of a *transcendental history*, which in a sense constitutes the *a priori* limit and structure of all historical knowledge.

It is on this model that we must view the relationship between language and a pure, transcendental experience which, like human infancy, is free both of the subject and of any psychological substratum. It is not simply an event to be isolated chronologically, nor anything like a psychosomatic state which either child psychology (at the level of *parole*) or palaeo-anthropology (at the level of *langue*) could ever construct as a human event independent of language. However, it is not even something that can be wholly resolved within language, except as a transcendental source or an Ur-limit in the sense already referred to. *In terms of human infancy, experience is the simple difference between the human and the linguistic. The individual as not already speaking, as having been and still being an infant – this is experience.* But that there is in this sense an infancy of the individual, that there is a difference between the human and linguistic, is not an event on a par with others in the realm of human history, or a simple characteristic among many that identify the species *Homo sapiens*. Infancy has its effect first and foremost on language, constituting it and conditioning it in an essential way. For the very fact that infancy exists as such – that it is, in other words, experience as the transcendental limit of language – rules out language as being in itself totality and truth. If there was no experience, if there was no infancy, language would undoubtedly be a 'game' in Wittgenstein's sense, its truth coinciding with its correct usage according to logical rules. But from the point where there is experience, where there is infancy, whose expropriation is the subject of language, then language appears as the place where experience must become truth. In other words infancy as Ur-limit in language emerges through constituting it as the site of truth. What Wittgenstein posits, at the end of the *Tractatus*, as the 'mystical' limit of language is not a psychic reality located outside or beyond language in some nebulous so-called 'mystical experience', it is the very transcendental origin of language, nothing other than infancy. *The ineffable is, in reality, infancy.* Experience is the *mystērion* which every individual intuits from the fact of having an infancy. This mystery is not an oath of silence or mystical ineffability; on the contrary, it is the vow that commits the individual to speech and to truth. Just as infancy destines language to truth, so language constitutes truth as the destiny of experience. Truth is not thereby something that can be defined within language, nor even outside it, as a given fact or as an 'equation' between this and language: infancy, truth and language are limited and constituted respectively in a primary, historico-transcendental relation in the sense already noted.

But infancy has another, more decisive consequence for language. It sets up in language that split between *language* and *discourse* which exclusively and fundamentally characterizes human language. For the fact that there is a difference between language (*langue*) and speech (*parole*), and that it is possible to pass from one to the other, and that each speaking individual is the site of this difference and this passage, is neither natural nor self-evident, but the central phenomenon of human language. Only now, thanks once more to Benveniste's studies, do we begin to discern this problematic, and its importance as the essential task with which any future science of language will be put to the test. It is not language in general that marks out the human from other living beings – according to the Western metaphysical tradition that sees man as a *zōon lógon échon* (an animal endowed with speech) – but the split between language and speech, between semiotic and semantic (in Benveniste's sense), between sign system and discourse. Animals are not in fact denied language; on the contrary, they are always and totally language. In them *la voix sacrée de la terre ingénue* (the sacred voice of the unknowing earth) – which Mallarmé, hearing the chirp of a cricket, sets against the human voice as *une* and *non-décomposée* (one and indivisible) – knows no breaks or interruptions. Animals do not enter language, they are already inside it. Man, instead, by having an infancy, by preceding speech, splits this single language and, in order to speak, has to constitute himself as the subject of language – he has to say *I*. Thus, if language is truly man's nature (and nature, on reflection, can only mean language without speech, *génesis synechés*, 'continuous origin', by Aristotle's definition, and to be nature means being always-already inside language), then man's nature is split at its source, for infancy brings it discontinuity and the difference between language and discourse.

The historicity of the human being has its basis in this difference and discontinuity. Only because of this is there history, only because of this is man a historical being – only because there is a human infancy, only because language is not the same as the human, and there is a difference between language and discourse, semiotic and semantic. For pure language is in itself ahistorical, and nature in the absolute has no need of a history. Imagine a man born already equipped with language, a man who already possessed speech. For such a man without infancy, language would not be a pre-existing thing to be appropriated, and for him there would be neither any break between language and speech nor any historicity of language. But such a man would thereby at once be united with his nature; his nature would always pre-exist, and nowhere in it would he find any discontinuity, any difference through which any kind of history could be produced. Like the animal, whom Marx describes as 'immediately at one with its life activity',[7] he would merge with it and would never be able to see it as an object distinct from himself.

It is infancy, it is the transcendental experience of the difference between language and speech, which first opens the space of history. Thus Babel – that is, the exit from the Eden of pure language and the entry into the babble of infancy (when, linguists tell us, the baby forms the phonemes of every language in the world) – is the transcendental origin of history. In this sense, to experience necessarily means to re-accede to infancy as history's transcendental place of origin. The enigma which infancy ushered in for man can be dissolved only in history, just as experience, being infancy and human place of origin, is something he is always in the act of falling from, into language and into speech. History, therefore, cannot be the continuous progress of speaking humanity through linear time, but in its essence is hiatus, discontinuity, *epochē*. That which has its place of origin in infancy must keep on travelling towards and through infancy.

GLOSSES

I Infancy and Language
The theory of infancy, as man's original historico-transcendental dimension, becomes most meaningful when it is related to the

category of the science of language: specifically, Benveniste's distinction between *semiotic* and *semantic*, which this theory can coherently develop.

It is through this distinction that Benveniste can establish a fundamental division within language, one that is now well known and very different from Saussure's categories of *langue* and *parole*. Whereas Saussure's distinction between language and speech is usually construed simply as a distinction between the collective and the individual, between the 'symphony' and its 'execution' in phonation, Benveniste's distinction is more complex. It touches on the question of the transition from language to discourse, a question dramatically posed by Saussure in a manuscript as yet unpublished; here he states that language exists only in relation to discourse, and asks what separates discourse from language; or rather, what allows us to say that at a given moment language becomes activated as discourse. Various concepts, he says, are latent in language (i.e. clothed in linguistic form), such as *ox, lake, sky, red, sad, five, sunder, see*. At what point and through what mechanism, what interplay, and under what conditions will these concepts form discourse? This series of words, richly evocative as they are, will never tell one human individual that another, by speaking them, wishes to communicate some meaning to him. This is the question which Benveniste takes on in a series of exemplary studies (*Les Niveaux de l'analyse linguistique*, 1964; *La Forme et le Sens dans le langage*, 1967; *Sémiologie de la langue*, 1969) which lead him to identify a *double signification* within language: two discrete and contrasting signifying modes, the semiotic and the semantic:

> The semiotic designates the signifying mode pertaining to the linguistic SIGN, constituting it as a unity. For the purposes of analysis, it is possible to consider separately the two sides of the sign, but within the signifying relation, unity it is and unity it remains. The only question prompted by a sign for its recognition is whether it exists, and this can be answered by a yes or a

no: *arbre – chanson – laver – nerf – jaune – sur*, not **orbre –
*vanson – *laner – *derf – *saune – *tur*. . . . Taken in itself, the
sign is pure correspondence with itself, and pure difference in
relation to any other sign. . . . It exists when it is recognized as a
signifier by all the members of the linguistic community. . . .
With the semantic, we enter into the specific mode of signification engendered by DISCOURSE. The questions that arise
here are a function of language as producer of messages. Now
the message is not reducible to a succession of units to be
separately identified; it is not the addition of signs which
produces meaning; rather, it is the meaning (the 'formulation')
in its total conception, which is enacted and which divides itself
into specific 'signs', which are WORDS. . . . The semantic order
corresponds to the world of enunciation and the universe of
discourse.

At issue are two distinct orders of ideas and two conceptual
universes, and this can be further shown by the difference in
criteria of validity required by the one and the other. The
semiotic (the sign) must be RECOGNIZED; the semantic (discourse) must be UNDERSTOOD. The difference between recognition and understanding entails two separate faculties of
the mind: the ability to perceive a correspondence between
what is there and what has been there before, and the ability
to perceive the meaning of a new enunciation. . . . The
semiotic marks a property of language, the semantic results
from the speaker's enactment of language. The semiotic sign
exists in itself, founding the reality of language, but it has no
specific application; the sentence, which expresses the semantic, can only be specific. . . . It is worth giving closer
consideration to this noteworthy fact, which seems to elucidate the theoretical articulation which we are struggling to
draw out. We can transpose the semantics of one language
into that of another, '*salva veritate*'; this is the potential for
translation. But we cannot transpose the semiotics of one
language into that of another; this is the non-potential for

translation. This is where the difference between semiotic and semantic lies.

Thus Benveniste articulates, in all its complexity, the question which Saussure had barely touched upon; and it is indeed Benveniste's recognition of its central importance that enabled him to lay the groundwork for a fertile new development of the science of language (think of the theory of enunciation, for example). But Saussure's question (what separates discourse from language, and at what point can we say that language becomes operative as discourse?) is no less relevant. In fact, Benveniste recognizes that the two orders, semiotic and semantic, remain separate and incommunicable, so that in theory there can be nothing to indicate the transition from one to the other: 'The world of the sign is closed. Between the sign and the sentence there is no transition, neither through syntagmatization nor otherwise. A moat separates them.' If this is true, Saussure's question is merely reformulated, becoming: why is human language like this, with this moat at its source? Why is there a double signification?

The theory of infancy allows a coherent response to this problem. The historico-transcendental dimension which this term designates occupies this very site of the 'moat' between semiotic and semantic, between pure language and discourse, and could be said to explain it. It is the fact of man's infancy (in other words, in order to speak, he need to be constituted as a subject within language by removing himself from infancy) which breaks the closed world of the sign and transforms pure language into human discourse, the semiotic into the semantic. Because of his infancy, because he does not speak from the very start, man cannot enter into language as a system of signs without radically transforming it, without constituting it in discourse.

It thus becomes clear in what sense Benveniste's 'double signification' should be construed. Semiotic and semantic are not in substance two realities but are, rather, the two transcendental limits which define and simultaneously are defined by man's infancy. The semiotic is nothing other than the pure pre-babble language of nature, in which man shares in order to speak, but from which the Babel of infancy perpetually withdraws him. The semantic does not exist except in its momentary emergence from the semiotic in the instance of discourse, whose elements, once uttered, fall back into pure language, which reassembles them in its mute dictionary of signs. Like dolphins, for a mere instant human language lifts its head from the semiotic sea of nature. But the human is nothing other than this very passage from pure language to discourse; and this transition, this instant, is history.

II Nature and Culture, or the Double Inheritance

The opposition between nature and culture, which continues to be the subject of such lively debate between philosophers and anthropologists, immediately becomes clearer if it is translated into the familiar biological terms of endosomatic and esosomatic inheritance. From this perspective nature can only mean the inheritance transmitted through the genetic code, while culture is the inheritance transmitted through non-genetic vehicles, the most important of which is undoubtedly language. *Homo sapiens* can thus be defined as the living species which is characterized by a double inheritance, whereby natural language (the genetic code) exists in tandem with an esosomatic language (cultural tradition). But if we go no further than these considerations, we risk over-looking what is at the very heart of the problem: the complexity of interrelations between the two forms of inheritance, one that can in no way be reduced to a simple opposition.

First and foremost, it should be noted that the most recent studies on language tend to show that it is not entirely a property of the esosomatic sphere. Alongside Chomsky's reformulation of ideas on innate linguistic capacities, Lenneberg has sought to elucidate the biological foundations of language. Certainly, in contrast with what occurs in the majority of animal species (and in terms of what Bentley and Hoy recently demonstrated for the chirp of the cricket, in which we can therefore truly see, with

Mallarmé, *la voix une et non décomposée* of nature), human language is not wholly written into the genetic code. Thorpe's observation that certain birds deprived at an early stage of the possibility of hearing the song of creatures of the same species produce the normal song only partially, means that to a certain extent they can be said to need to learn it; in the human individual, exposure to language is indispensable for the acquisition of language. It is a fact whose importance can never be overemphasized in understanding the structure of human language that if a child is not exposed to speech between the ages of two and twelve, his or her potential for language acquisition is definitively jeopardized. Contrary to ancient traditional beliefs, from this point of view man is not the 'animal possessing language', but instead the animal deprived of language and obliged, therefore, to receive it from outside himself.

On the other hand, alongside this information illuminating the esosomatic aspect of language, other elements lead us to suppose that language also belongs partly to the endosomatic sphere: like the concurrence in the chronological stages of language acquisition among children throughout the world, noted by Jakobson, or the imbalance between received linguistic information and the linguistic competence of the child, to which Chomsky has drawn attention. But there is no need to think in terms of language as being inscribed in the genetic code, nor has anything like a language gene been identified so far. What is certain is that, as Lenneberg has shown, while in the majority of animal species communicative behaviour invariably develops according to pre-established laws of genetic maturation, so that the animal will ultimately have command of a repertoire of signals characteristic of the species, in the human a separation has come about between predisposition to language (readiness for communication) and the process of realizing this potentiality. In other words, human language is split at its source into an endosomatic sphere and an esosomatic sphere, between which there is (or can be) set up a phenomenon of resonance which produces its actualization. If there is no exposure to the esosomatic inheritance during a certain phase of brain cell development (which, according to Lenneberg, has its upper limit in the full development of the cerebral hemispheres around the age of twelve), then linguistic capacity is irretrievably lost.

If this is true, the duality of the endosomatic and esosomatic inheritances, of nature and culture in the human species, can be understood in a new way. It is not a matter of juxtaposing two distinct and unconnected spheres, but of a doubleness which is already inscribed in that very language which has always been regarded as the basis of culture. What marks human language is not its belonging to either the esosomatic or the endosomatic sphere, but its situation, so to speak, on the cusp of the two, and its consequent articulation within both their difference and their resonance. From this perspective the binary oppositions which are found at every level of language – between language and discourse, between the unconscious phonomatic level and the semantic level of discourse, between form and sense – acquire specific significance. Split as it is between an esosomatic and an endosomatic inheritance, human language must necessarily have a structure that permits the passage from one to the other. If we return to Thom's image of two linear oscillators which resonate, we see that these, though distinct, exhibit common properties enabling the phenomenon of resonance; but once resonance is established, the two systems lose their independence and form a single system (the resonant system). We can likewise conceive of endosomatic and esosomatic, nature and culture, as two distinct systems which, resonating in language, produce a single new system. There must, however, be a mediating element which enables the two systems to resonate. This element is what Jakobson described as the phonomatic level of language (or, in learning terms, what Chomsky constructs as universal generative grammar).

The fact that Jakobson displaces the question of the phoneme's *mode* and *site* of existence on to ontology then ceases to appear as merely an ironic procedure. Phonemes, those differential signs that are both 'pure and empty' and 'signifying and non-signifying', do not strictly belong either to the semiotic or the semantic, language or discourse, form or sense, endosomatic or esosomatic; they are located in the correspondence-difference (in the *chōra*, as Plato would have said) between the two regions, in a 'site' which can perhaps be described only in its topology and which coincides with that historico-transcendental region – before the subject of language and without somatic substance – which we have defined above as human *infancy*.

Structured thus on the difference between endosomatic and esosomatic, between nature and culture, language gives resonance to the two systems and enables their communication. It is this position *on the boundary* between two simultaneously continuous and discontinuous dimensions which makes human language able to transcend the purely semiotic sphere and acquire, in Benveniste's words, a 'double signification'.

Every language that is wholly contained within a single dimension (whether it is the chirp of the cricket or sign systems employed by man other than language) necessarily remains within the semiotic, and its functioning requires that it be merely *recognized*, not *comprehended*. Only human language, as something belonging to both the endosomatic and the esosomatic, adds another sense to semiotic meaning, transforming the closed world of the sign into the open world of semantic expression. So human language, as Jakobson observes, is the only sign system composed of elements (phonemes) which – precisely because, as we have seen, they enable the passage from the semiotic to the semantic – are simultaneously signifying and non-signifying.

Human infancy – in which we have identified the origins of experience and of history – therefore acquires its true meaning when it is placed in the context of the difference between esosomatic and endosomatic inheritance in the human species.

III *Lévi-Strauss and the Language of Babel*
Locating infancy thus between pure language and human language, between semiotic and semantic, gives us a new way of

understanding the meaning of a body of work which has fundamentally revivified the human sciences in our time: that of Lévi-
Strauss. This is because Lévi-Strauss's conception of human
actions is marked by his decision to make sense of them wholly
on the level of pure language – that is, on a level where there is no
hiatus, no infancy between language and discourse, semiotic and
semantic. (It is not accidental that the model for his researches
should derive from phonology, a science which is exclusively
situated at the level of *langue*.) This lack of any break between
language and discourse explains how, in an analysis whose perti-
nence has been acknowledged by Lévi-Strauss himself, Ricoeur
was able to define his thought as a 'Kantism without a transcendental subject', and to speak about structures in terms of 'an
unconscious more Kantian than Freudian, a categorical, combinatory unconscious . . . a categorical system that does not refer to
a thinking subject . . . analogous to nature'. Because that source of
origin which, from Descartes on, was sought by philosophers in
the subject of language, is found by Lévi-Strauss instead (and this
is his genius) with a leap beyond the subject, into the pure
language of nature. But for this he needs an engine, which, by
translating human discourse into pure language, can allow him to
pass from the one to the other without a split. The Lévi-Straussian
conception of myth is such an engine. In myth Lévi-Strauss sees an
intermediary dimension between language and speech:

> Myth is a verbal entity which, within the sphere of language,
> occupies a position akin to that of the crystal in the world of
> physical matter. In relation to language [*langue*], on the one
> hand, and speech [*parole*], on the other, its position indeed
> resembles that of the crystal: an intermediary object between a
> statistical aggregate of molecules and the molecular structure
> itself.

The implicit suggestion in Lévi-Strauss's characterization of myth
as 'the mode of discourse in which the formula *traduttore, traditore*

has practically no meaning' is that myth thus comes to occupy a median sphere between the opposition of semiotic and semantic, which Benveniste has indeed characterized as the opposition between the possibility and impossibility of translation.

It could be said that in this sense Lévi-Strauss's entire œuvre is an engine which transforms human language into *pre-Babel* language; history into nature. This is why his analyses, which are so illuminating on the subject of the passage from discourse to language (that is, on the subject of what could be defined as nature *in* man), are somewhat less useful on the subject of the passage from language to discourse (what could be defined as the nature *of* man). From this point of view, *infancy is precisely the reverse engine, transforming pure pre-Babel language into human discourse, nature into history.*

IV Infancy and Mystery

Within the perspective of infancy as a source of the human, the essence of mystical experience in Antiquity becomes perhaps more comprehensible than has been variously explained by scholars. For if we know that, as *páthēma*, it was ultimately an anticipation of death (Plutarch tells us that to die, *teleutān*, and to be initiated, *teleísthai*, are one and the same thing), the very element which all the sources concur in seeing as essence, and from which the very name 'mystery' derives (from **mu*, which indicates the moaning sound when the mouth is closed) – in other words, silence – it is what has as yet found no adequate explanation. If it is true that in its primary form, what was at the heart of the experience of the mysteries was not a knowing, but a suffering (in Aristotle's words, '*ou matheīn, allà patheīn*'), and if this *páthēma* was in its essence abstracted from language – was an un-speakable, a closed-mouthed moaning – then this experience approximated an experience of infancy in the sense we have seen (the fact that toys – *puerilia ludicra* – featured among the sacred symbols of initiation could accordingly be a useful area of inquiry).

But certainly during the period about which we know most

(when the mysteries were at their height, from the fourth century AD onwards), and probably earlier, the ancient world interprets this mysterical infancy as a knowledge which cannot be spoken of, as a silence to be kept. So, as they appear in Giamblico's *De Mysteriis*, the mysteries are now a 'teurgia', essentially a skill, a 'technique' for influencing the gods. Here the *páthēma* becomes *máthēma*, the un-speakable of infancy, a secret doctrine weighed down by an oath of esoteric silence.

This is why it is the fable, something which can only be narrated, and not the mystery, which must not be spoken of, which contains the truth of infancy as man's source of origin. For in the fairy tale man is freed from the mystery's obligation of silence by transforming it into enchantment: it is not participation in a cult of knowledge which renders him speechless, but bewitchment. The silence of the mystery is undergone as a rupture, plunging man back into the pure, mute language of nature; but as a spell, silence must eventually be shattered and conquered. This is why, in the fairy tale, man is struck dumb, and animals emerge from the pure language of nature in order to speak. Through the temporary confusion of the two spheres, it is the world of the *open mouth*, of the Indo-European root **bha* (from which the word fable is derived), which the fairy tale validates, against the world of the *closed mouth*, of the root **mu*.

The medieval definition of the fable, whereby it is a narration in which 'animalia muta . . . sermocinasse finguntur' and, as such, something essentially 'contra naturam', contains a great deal more truth than might at first appear. Indeed, it can be said that the fairy tale is the place where, through the inversion of the categories: closed mouth/open mouth, pure language/infancy, man and nature exchange roles before each finds their own place in history.

Notes

One

1. Walter Benjamin, 'The Storyteller', in *Illuminations*, transl. Harry Zohn, Glasgow: Fontana 1973.
2. Walter Benjamin, 'On the Program of the Coming Philosophy' (1917/18), transl. Mark Ritter, in Gary Smith (ed.), *Benjamin: Philosophy, Aesthetics, History*, Chicago: University of Chicago Press 1989, pp. 1–2.

Two

1. Francis Bacon, *Novum Organum*, London: William Pickering 1844, p. 60.
2. 'Unformed, without a shape to be worked upon.'
3. 'There is no constancy in existence, neither of our being, nor that of objects. . . . Thus nothing certain can be averred about the one or the other . . .'
4. 'So excellently managing time that they have tried to savour death itself, and have strained their minds to apprehend this crossing over; but they did not return to give us news of it.'
5. 'Archimedes asked only to have one point fixed and stable.'
6. 'But what of those which I attributed to the vital force, as being nourished, or walking? Since I now have no body, these two are nothing but fictions. Sensation? Certainly this likewise does not take place without a body, and there are many things I have seemed to be sensible of in dreams which afterwards I perceived not to have been sensations of mine. Thinking? Here I have it, – it is thought; this alone cannot be torn away from me . . .' Descartes, Second Meditation, *Meditations*, 1878 edn, transl. Richard Lowndes.
7. '. . . we must at last confidently pronounce this conclusion: 'I am, I exist,' so often as I declare it or think it, must necessarily be true . . . 'I am, I exist' is certain. For how long, though? Certainly, for so long as I think: for, perchance it might be that if I were to cease from all thinking I might thereupon wholly cease to be –' (ibid.)

8. '. . . a thinking thing, that is, a mind, or soul, or intelligence, or reason . . .' (ibid.)
9. '. . . a thing that thinks: what is this? Clearly, one that doubts, understands, affirms, denies, wills, refuses, imagines too, and feels' (ibid.)
10. 'without imagination, man has no possibility of understanding.'
11. G.W.F. Hegel, *Phenomenology of Spirit*, transl. A.V. Miller, Oxford: Clarendon Press 1977, p. 109.
12. ibid., pp. 115–16.
13. A. Baillet, *Vie de M. Descartes*, Paris 1691.

Three

1. I. Kant, *Critique of Pure Reason*, transl. J.M.D. Meiklejohn, London: Everyman's Library 1934, p. 236.
2. Hegel, *Phenomenology*, pp. 55–6.
3. ibid., p. 493.
4. G. von Leibniz, *Discourse on Metaphysics, Correspondence with Arnauld and Monadology*, transl. George R. Montgomery, Chicago: Open Court 1902, p. 254.
5. H. Bergson, *Essai sur les données immédiates de la conscience*, in *Oeuvres*, vol. 1, Paris: Presses Universitaires de France 1959.
6. E. Husserl, *Cartesian Meditations*, transl. Dorian Cairns, Martinus Nijhoff, The Hague 1960.
7. M. de Montaigne, *The Essays*, Florio translation, 1886 edition, pp. 184–8.
8. J.-J. Rousseau, *Reveries of the Solitary Walker*, transl. Peter France, Harmondsworth: Penguin 1979, pp. 38–9.
9. R.M. Rilke, *The Duino Elegies*, transl. J.B. Leishman and Stephen Spender, London: Hogarth 1939.

Four

1. E. Husserl, *Origin of Geometry*, introduction by J. Derrida, transl. John P. Leavey Jr, Brighton: Nicholas Hayes/Harvester Press 1978, p. 161.
2. ibid., p. 162.
3. ibid.
4. ibid., p. 161.
5. E. Benveniste, *Problèmes de linguistique générale*, Paris: Gallimard 1972, pp. 260, 262.
6. ibid., p. 261.
7. K. Marx, *Economic and Philosophical Manuscripts of 1844*, in *Marx-Engels Collected Works*, vol. 3, transl. Martin Milligan and Dirk J. Struik, London: Lawrence & Wishart 1975, p. 276.

IN PLAYLAND

Reflections on History and Play

To Claude Lévi-Strauss
in respectful homage for his seventieth birthday

Everyone knows the bit in Collodi's novel where Pinocchio, having travelled through the night on the back of the talking donkey, arrives happily at dawn in 'Playland'. In his description of this infantile utopian republic, Collodi has left us the image of a universe where there is nothing but play:

It was a country unlike any other country in the world. The population was composed entirely of boys. The oldest were fourteen, and the youngest scarcely eight years old. In the street there was such merriment, noise and shouting, that it was enough to turn anybody's head. There were troops of boys everywhere. Some were playing with nuts, some with battle-dores, some with balls. Some rode velocipedes, others wooden horses. A party were playing at hide and seek, a few were chasing one another. Boys dressed in straw were eating lighted tow; some were reciting, some singing, some leaping. Some were amusing themselves with walking on their hands with their feet in the air; others were trundling hoops, or strutting about dressed as generals, wearing leaf helmets and command-ing a squadron of cardboard soldiers. Some were laughing, some shouting some were calling out; others clapped their hands, or whistled, or clucked like a hen who has just laid an egg. To sum it all up, it was such a pandemonium, such a bedlam, such an uproar, that not to be deafened it would have been necessary to stuff one's ears with cotton wool. In every square canvas theatres had been erected . . .[1]

The immediate result of this invasion of life by play is a change and acceleration of time: 'in the midst of continual games and every variety of amusement, the hours, the days, and the weeks passed like lightning'. As was to be expected, the acceleration of time does not leave the calendar unaltered. The calendar, whose essence is rhythm, alternation and repetition, is now stopped short in the measureless dilation of one long holiday. 'Every week' – Lampwick explains to Pinocchio – 'is made up of six Thursdays and a Sunday. Just think that the autumn holiday begins on the first of January and ends the last day of December.'

If we are to believe Lampwick's words, the 'pandemonium', the 'uproar' and the 'bedlam' of Playland result, therefore, in the paralysis and destruction of the calendar.

It is worth dwelling on Lampwick's explanation. We know in fact that in ancient times, and still in the present among so-called primitive peoples (which we should rather call, as Lévi-Strauss suggested, cold societies or societies where history is frozen), 'pandemonium', 'uproar' and 'bedlam' had instead the function of instituting and securing the stability of the calendar. Let us consider that group of rituals – common to diverse cultures, widely separated by time and space – which ethnographers and historians of religion call 'New Year ceremonies', which are characterized by orgiastic disorder, the suspension or subversion of social hierarchies, and licence of every kind, whose object, in every case, is to ensure both the regeneration of time and the fixity of the calendar. We have a description of the ceremony known as No, with which the ancient Chinese celebrated the enthronement of the twelve genies which were to preside over the months of the new year.

> 'I myself have seen [writes Lieou Yu, a man of letters who found this custom unseemly] on every night of the full moon of the first month, streets and alleys filled with people, where the dinning of drums deafened the heavens and torches illumined the earth. The people wear animal masks and the men dress as women; minstrels and jugglers are garbed outlandishly. Men

and women go together to see this, and they mingle instead of avoiding one another. They squander their wealth, and destroy their portion of inheritance . . .'[2]

Frazer describes the old Scottish festival known as *calluinn* (bacchanal) which took place on the last day of the year, when a man dressed in a cowhide and followed by a clamorous crowd of boys, who would make the hide resound by beating sticks against it, went round every house three times in imitation of the sun's path. Likewise *akîtu*, the Babylonian New Year festival, whose first phase implied a return to primordial chaos and a subversion of social order, approximated the 'festival of the fates' [*zakmuk*], in which auguries for each of the twelve months of the year were determined; *naurôz*, the Persian New Year, was also the day on which the settling of human destinies for an entire year took place.

The conclusions that could be drawn from comparing such diverse rituals within such heterogeneous cultures are unlikely to have any scientific validity. Rather, it can be noted that this relation between rites and the calendar does not apply only to New Year rituals. The functional relationship between rites and calendar is generally so close that Lévi-Strauss was able to write in a recent study: 'rites fix the stages of the calendar, as localities do those of an itinerary. The latter furnish extension, the former duration'; and that 'the real function of ritual is . . . to preserve the continuity of lived experience'.[2]

If this is true, and Lampwick's reflections are still to be taken seriously, we can hypothesize a relation of both correspondence and opposition between play and ritual, in the sense that both are engaged in a relationship with the calendar and with time, but this relationship is in each case an inverse one: ritual fixes and *structures* the calendar; play, on the other hand, though we do not yet know how and why, changes and *destroys* it.

The hypothesis of an inverse relationship between play and rite is really less arbitrary than may seem at first sight. Scholars have long known that the realms of play and of the sacred are closely linked. Numerous well-documented researches show that the origins of most of the games known to us lie in ancient sacred ceremonies, in dances, ritual combat and divinatory practices. So in ball games we can discern the relics of the ritual representation of a myth in which the gods fought for possession of the sun; the circle game was an ancient matrimonial rite; games of chance derive from oracular practices; the spinning-top and the chequered board were tools of divination.

In a study by Benveniste which occupies a singular place in the great linguist's bibliography, he took the anthropologists' conclusions as a point of departure, and elaborated this relation between play and ritual, asking not only what they have in common, but also how they differ. For if it is true that play derives from the realm of the sacred, it is also true that it radically transforms it – indeed, overturns it to the point where it can plausibly be defined as 'topsy-turvy sacred'. 'The potency of the sacred act', writes Benveniste,

> resides precisely in the conjunction of the *myth* that articulates history and the *ritual* that reproduces it. If we make a comparison between this schema and that of play, the difference appears fundamental: in play only the ritual survives and all that is preserved is the *form* of the sacred drama, in which each element is re-enacted time and again. But what has been forgotten or abolished is the myth, the meaningfully worded fabulation that endows the acts with their sense and their purpose.[3]

Analogous considerations apply to the *jocus*, i.e. wordplay: 'in contrast to the *ludus*, but in a symmetrical manner, the *jocus* consists in a pure *myth*, to which there is no corresponding *ritual* that can connect it to reality'. These considerations furnish Benveniste with the elements of a definition of play as structure: 'it has its source in the sacred, of which it supplies a broken, topsy-turvy image. If the sacred can be defined as the con-substantial unity of myth and ritual, we can say that play exists when only one half of the sacred enactment is fulfilled, translating myth alone into words and ritual alone into actions'.[4]

The inverse link between play and the sacred that Lampwick's considerations had suggested is shown, then, to be substantially accurate. Playland is a country whose inhabitants are busy celebrating rituals, and manipulating objects and sacred words, whose sense and purpose they have, however, forgotten. And we should not be amazed if, through this oblivion, through the dismemberment and inversion of which Benveniste speaks, they free the sacred, too, from its link with the calendar and with the cyclical rhythm of time that it sanctions, thereby entering another dimension of time, where the hours go by in a flash and the days are changeless.

In play, man frees himself from sacred time and 'forgets' it in human time.

But the world of play is connected to time in an even more specific sense. We have seen that everything pertaining to play once pertained to the realm of the sacred. But this does not exhaust the realm of play. Indeed, human beings keep on inventing games, and it is also possible to play with what once pertained to the practical-economic sphere. A look at the world of toys shows that children, humanity's little scrap-dealers, will play with whatever junk comes their way, and that play thereby preserves profane objects and behaviour that have ceased to exist. Everything which is old, independent of its sacred origins, is liable to become a toy. What is more, the same appropriation and transformation in play (the same *illusion*, one could say, restoring to the word its etymological meaning, from *in-ludere*) can be achieved – for example, by means of miniaturization – in relation to objects which still belong in the sphere of use: a car, a pistol, an electric cooker are at once transformed into toys, thanks to miniaturization. But what, then, is the essence of the toy? The essential character of the toy – the only one, on reflection, that can distinguish it from other objects – is something quite singular, which can be grasped only in the temporal dimension of a 'once upon a time' and a 'no more' (presupposing, however, as the example of the miniature demonstrates, that this 'once upon a time' and this 'no more' be understood not only in a *diachronic* sense, but also in a *synchronic* sense). The toy is what belonged – *once, no longer* – to the realm of the sacred or of the practical-economic. But if this is true, the essence of the toy (that 'soul of the toy' which, Baudelaire tells us, is what babies vainly seek to grasp when they fidget with their toys, shake them, throw them on the ground, pull them apart and finally reduce them to shreds) is, then, an eminently *historical* thing: indeed it is, so to speak, the Historical in its pure state. For in the toy, as in no other site, can we grasp the temporality of history in its pure differential and qualitative value. Not in a monument, an object of archaeological and scholarly research, which preserves in time its practical, documentary character (its 'material content', Benjamin would have said); not in an antique, whose value is a function of its quantitative ageing; not in an archive document, which draws its value from its place in a chronology and a relationship of proximity and legality with the past event. The toy represents something more and something different from all these things. It has often been asked what is left of the model after its transformation into a toy, for it is certainly not a matter of its cultural significance, nor of its function, nor even of its form (which can be perfectly reproduced or altered almost beyond recognition, as anyone who is familiar with the elastic iconism of toys knows very well). What the toy preserves of its sacred or economic model, what survives of this after its dismemberment or miniaturization, is nothing other than the human temporality that was contained therein: its pure historical essence. The toy is a materialization of the historicity contained in objects, extracting it by means of a particular manipulation. While the value and meaning of the antique object and the document are functions of their age – that is, of their making present and rendering tangible a relatively remote past – the toy, dismembering and distorting the past or miniaturizing the present – playing as much on *diachrony* as on *synchrony* – makes present and renders tangible human temporality in itself, the pure differential margin between the 'once' and the 'no longer'.

Seen in this light, the toy presents certain analogies with *bricolage*, the concept used by Lévi-Strauss in what are now classic pages to illustrate how mythic thought proceeds. Like *bricolage*, the toy, too, uses 'crumbs' and 'scraps' belonging to other structural wholes (or, at any rate modified structural wholes); and the toy, too, thereby transforms old signifieds into signifiers, and vice versa. But what it 'plays' with are not simply these crumbs and scraps, but – as the case of miniaturization makes clear – the 'crumbness', if one can put it that way, which is contained in a temporal form within the object or the structural whole from which it departs. From this perspective the meaning of miniaturization as a figure of the toy is shown to be wider than that which Lévi-Strauss confers on it when he identifies in the 'reduced model' (broadly speaking) what *bricolage* has in common with the work of art. For here miniaturization stands not so much for what it allows to be known of the whole before the parts, or for the conquest, in a single rapacious glance, of what is to be feared in the object ('La poupée de l'enfant n'est plus un adversaire, un rival ou même un interlocuteur . . .' – now the child's doll is not an adversary, a rival, or even an interlocutor), so much as allowing the pure temporality contained in the object to be grasped and enjoyed. *Miniaturization is, in other words, the cipher of history.* Thus it is not so much the *bricoleur* as the collector who naturally appears as the figure closest to the player. For just as antique objects are collected, so are miniatures of objects. But in both cases the collector extracts the object from its diachronic distance or its synchronic proximity and gathers it into the remote adjacence of history – into what, to paraphrase one of Benjamin's definitions, could be defined as 'une citation à l'ordre du jour', on the final day of history.

If this is true – if what children play with is history, and if play is a relationship with objects and human behaviour that draws from them a pure historical-temporal aspect – it does not then seem irrelevant that in a fragment of Heraclitus – that is to say, at the origins of European thought – *aiōn*, time in its original sense, should figure as a 'child playing with dice', and that 'domain of the baby' should define the scope of this play. Etymologists reduce the word *aiōn* to a root *ai-w, which means 'vital force', and this, they say, is the meaning that *aiōn* would have had in its most ancient instances in the Homeric texts, before taking on that of 'spinal marrow' and, finally, by a somewhat inexplicable passage, that of 'duration' and 'eternity'. In fact, if we take a closer look at the Homeric value of this term, we see that *aiōn* is often yoked to *psychē* in expressions of the kind: '*psychē* and *aiōn* abandoned him', to indicate death. If *psychē* is the vital principle which animates the body, what can be the sense here of its conjoining with *aiōn*, except to prompt a simple repetition? *Aiōn* (this is the only interpretation which makes it possible to reduce these various meanings to a coherent whole) indicates vital force in so far as this is perceived in the living being as a temporal thing, as something that 'endures'; that is, as the *temporalizing essence* of the living being, while *psychē* is the breath that animates the body and *thumós* is what moves the limbs. When Heraclitus tells us that *aiōn* is a child playing, he thereby depicts as play the temporalizing essence of the living being – his or her 'historicity', we could say (even if the translation 'history is a child playing' would certainly be a doubtful one).

Along with *aiōn*, to indicate time the Greek language also conceives the term *chrónos*, indicating an objective duration, a measurable and continuous quantity of time. In a famous passage in the *Timaeus*, Plato presents the relationship between *chrónos* and *aiōn* as a relationship of copy and model, of cyclical time measured by the movements of the stars and motionless, synchronic temporality. What interests us here is not so much that in the process of a still living translation *aiōn* should be identified with eternity and *chrónos* with diachronic time as that our culture should conceive from its very origins a split between two different, correlated and opposed notions of time.

We can now return to the relationship of correspondence and opposition which we have seen connecting play and rite, and to their inverse situation in relation to time and the calendar. In a passage from *La Pensée sauvage* on adoption rites among the Fox Indians,[5] Lévi-Strauss drew the opposition between ritual and play into an exemplary formula: while rites transform events into structures, play transforms structures into events. Developing this definition in the light of these considerations, we can state that the function of rites is to adjust the contradiction between mythic past and present, annulling the interval separating them and reabsorbing all events into the synchronic structure. Play, on the other hand, furnishes a symmetrically opposed operation: it tends to break the connection between past and present, and to break down and crumble the whole structure into events. If ritual is therefore a machine for transforming diachrony into synchrony, play, conversely, is a machine for transforming synchrony into diachrony.

From the perspective which interests us here, we can consider this a precise definition, though modifying it with the clarification that in either case this transformation is never complete – not only because however far back we go in time, and however much we extend ethnographic exploration, we always find play alongside ritual and ritual alongside play, but also because every game, as already noted, contains a ritual aspect and every rite an aspect of play, which often makes it awkward to distinguish one from the other. Kerényi observed, in relation to Greek and Roman ceremonies, that the 'quotation' of myth within life which they enacted always implied a ludic element. When Juvenal wishes to characterize the impiety of an obscene secret cult among Roman women, he writes: 'Nil ibi per ludum simulabitur oblique omnia fient ad verum' ('No make-believe here, no pretence': *Satires*), as if religious *pietas* and ludic attitude were the same thing.[6] And Huizinga was easily able to find examples of how ritual behaviour often betrays an awareness of 'make-believe' which harks back to the player's awareness of playing. Ritual and play appear, rather, as two tendencies operating in every society, although the one never has the effect of eliminating the other, and although one might prevail over the other to a varying degree, they always maintain a differential margin between diachrony and synchrony.

The definition we cited above must, then, be corrected inasmuch as ritual and play are both machines for producing differential margins between diachrony and synchrony, even if this is effected by an inverse movement in the two cases. Indeed, to be more precise, *we can regard ritual and play not as two distinct machines but as a single machine, a single binary system, which is articulated across two categories which cannot be isolated and across whose correlation and difference the very functioning of the system is based.*

From this structural correlation between ritual and play, between diachrony and synchrony, we can draw significant conclusions. For if human societies appear in this light as a single system traversed by two opposing tendencies, the one operating to transform diachrony into synchrony and the other impelled towards the contrary, the end result of the play of these tendencies – what is produced by the system, by human society – is in every case a differential margin between diachrony and synchrony: *history; in other words, human time.*

Thus we find ourselves in possession of elements which permit a definition of history unfettered by the ingenuous substantialization which a stubbornly ethnocentric perspective has maintained in the historical sciences. Indeed, historiography cannot presume to identify its own object in diachrony, almost as if this were a substantial objective reality, rather than being (as the critiques of Lévi-Strauss show) the result of a codification using a chronological matrix; it must, like every human science, renounce the illusion of having its object directly in *realia*, and instead figure its object in terms of signifying relations between two correlated and opposed orders: the object of history is not diachrony, but the opposition between diachrony and synchrony which characterizes every human society. If it figures historical becoming as a pure succession of events, as an absolute diachrony, it is then constrained, in order to salvage the coherence of the system, to assume a hidden synchrony operating in every precise instance (representing it as a causal law or as teleology), whose sense is revealed, however, only dialectically in the total social process. But the precise instance as an intersection of synchrony and diachrony (the absolute presence) is a pure myth, which Western metaphysics makes use of to guarantee the continuation of its own dual conception of time. It is not merely – as Jakobson showed for linguistics – that synchrony cannot be identified with the static nor diachrony with the dynamic, but that the pure event (absolute diachrony) and the pure structure (absolute synchrony) do not exist. Every historical event represents a differential margin between diachrony and synchrony, instituting a signifying relation between them. Historical becoming cannot, therefore, be represented as a diachronic axis, in which the points a, b, c, . . . n mark out the discrete instances in which synchrony and diachrony coincide: but, rather, as a hyperbolic curve which expresses a series of differential margins between diachrony and synchrony (hence, in respect of which, synchrony and diachrony constitute only two axes of asymptotic reference):

History – as all anthropologists now accept, and as historians have no trouble acknowledging – is not the exclusive patrimony of some peoples, compared with which other societies figure as peoples without history. This is not because all societies are within time, within diachrony, but because all societies produce differential margins between diachrony and synchrony; in all societies, what we have here called ritual and play work to establish signifying relations between diachrony and synchrony. Far from being identified with the diachronic *continuum*, from this perspective history is nothing other than the result of the relation between diachronic signifiers and synchronic signifiers produced incessantly by ritual and play – the 'play', as we could say, using a mechanical value of the term, which is found in many languages, between diachrony and synchrony:

Given this correlation, we can also apprehend a means of articulating the distinction between 'cold' societies, or historically stationary societies, and 'hot' societies, or historically cumulative societies, which, starting with Lévi-Strauss, has replaced the traditional distinction between historical societies and societies without history. 'Cold' societies are those in which the sphere of ritual tends to be enlarged at the expense of play; 'hot' societies are those in which the sphere of play tends to be enlarged at the expense of ritual:

If this casts history as a system transforming ritual into play and play into ritual, the difference between the two kinds of society is not so much qualitative as quantitative: only the predominance of one signifying order over the other defines the placing of a society as of one kind or the other. At one extreme of such a classification we would situate the case (a purely asymptotic case, in reality, since we know no examples of such a society) of a society in which all play had become ritual, all diachrony transformed into synchrony. In such a society, where the diachronic interval between past and present would have been totally transcended, human beings would live in an eternal present – in other words, in that changeless eternity which indeed many religions set out as the dwelling of the gods. At the opposite extreme we would situate the similarly ideal case of a society where all ritual had been eroded by play, and all structures disintegrated into events: it is 'Playland', where the hours go by in a flash – or, in Greek mythology, the absolute diachrony of infernal time, symbolized by Ixion's wheel and the toils of Sisyphus. In both cases there would be a lack of that differential margin between diachrony and synchrony in which we have identified human time – in other words, history.

In this sense, both hot societies and cold societies seem to be pursuing – in opposite directions – the same project, which could be defined (as it has been) as the 'abolition of history'. But for now, at least, although the former have managed to multiply the maximum number of diachronic signifiers, and the latter to reduce them to the minimum, no society has managed to carry out this project completely, founding a society entirely without a calendar, like Playland, Hades or even, in a sense, the society of the gods: in historically cumulative societies the linearity of time is always arrested by the calendrical alternation and repetition of holiday time; in historically stationary societies circularity is always interrupted by profane time.

The fact is that inherent in both ritual and play is an ineradicable residue, a stumbling block on which their project is doomed to founder. In a mere few pages of *La Pensée sauvage*, Lévi-Strauss produced a magisterial analysis of those stone or wooden objects known as *churinga*, with which the Aranda, a central Australian people, represent the body of an ancestor and which then, generation after generation, are solemnly presented to the individual in whom it is believed the ancestor is repeatedly reincarnated. According to Lévi-Strauss, the function and specific character of these objects derive from the fact that in a society like that of the Aranda, which privileges synchrony to the point where it even depicts the relationship between past and present in synchronic terms, the *churinga* have the purpose of compensating for diachronic impoverishment by representing the diachronic past in a tangible form.

> If our interpretation of the *churinga* is correct, [he writes] their sacred character derives from the function of diachronic signification which they alone can guarantee, within a system which, being classificatory, is entirely laid out in a synchrony within which even duration is subsumed. The *churinga* are the palpable witnesses to the mythic period: that alcheringa which without them could still be conceived of, but which could no longer be physically evidenced.[7]

Lévi-Strauss does not detail the mechanism through which the *churinga* manages to assume this function of signifying diachrony. This is anything but a simple mechanism. As a tangible presence of the mythic past, as 'palpable proof that the ancestor and his descendant are a single flesh', the *churinga* seems in fact to be a signifier more of absolute synchrony than of diachrony. But once the ritual transformation of diachrony into synchrony has taken place in the body of the new individual, *what was the signifier of absolute synchrony, now freed, becomes invested by the diachrony which has lost its signifier (the embryo of the new individual), and is turned around into the signifier of absolute diachrony.* Thus, contrary to what Lévi-Strauss maintains, there is no contradiction between the fact that the Aranda declare the *churinga* to be the body of the ancestor and the fact that the ancestor does not lose his own body when, at the moment of conception, he leaves the *churinga* for his new incarnation; quite simply, a single object is here invested with two opposing signifying functions, according to whether the ritual is or is not yet terminated. If this is true, the ritual transformation of diachrony into synchrony necessarily leaves a diachronic residue (of which the *churinga*, construed in the broad sense, is the cipher), and the most perfect system a society has devised to abolish diachrony still carries, right up to the end, a production of diachrony in the very object that has enabled this abolition.

As might be expected, play too presents us with an analogous phenomenon; play too has its unbudgeable stumbling block. Because the toy, as a representation of a pure temporal interval, is undoubtedly a signifier of absolute diachrony, of the prior transformation of a structure into an event. But here too this signifier, once freed, becomes unstable, and is invested with a contrary meaning; here too, *at the end of the game*, the toy turns around into its opposite and is presented as the synchronic residue which the game can no longer eliminate. For if the transformation of synchrony into diachrony were really complete, it would leave no traces, and the miniature would have to correspond with its model, just as, *at the ritual's termination*, the *churinga* would have to vanish, corresponding to the body of the individual in whom the ancestor has been reincarnated. This is why toys and ritual objects demand analogous behaviour: once the ritual and the game are over, these, being embarrassing residues, must be hidden and put away, for in a sense they constitute the tangible denial of what they have none the less helped to make possible (one can wonder, at this point, whether the sphere of art in our society has not been marked out as the lumber room for gathering in these 'unstable' signifiers, which do not properly belong either to synchrony or to diachrony, either to ritual or to play).

Ritual and play thereby figure – and it seems inevitably so – as operations acting on the *signifiers* of diachrony and synchrony, transforming the diachronic signifiers into synchronic signifiers, and vice versa. Everything occurs, though, as if the social system contained a safety lock intended to guarantee its binary structure:

when all the diachronic signifiers have become synchronic signifiers, these in turn become signifiers of diachrony, and thus assure the continuity of the system. The same thing happens the other way round.

This potential for inversion – which, under certain conditions, is inherent in signifiers of diachrony and synchrony – also permits an explanation for ceremonies – for example, funeral ceremonies – in which ritual and play have a singular proximity. Everyone will remember the lively and meticulous description of the games concluding Patroclus' funeral in canto XXIII of the *Iliad*. Achilles has kept watch all night beside the pyre on which his friend's body is being burned, calling out to his soul and pouring wine on the flames, or fiercely giving vent to his sorrow on the unburied corpse of Hector. Now, suddenly, grief gives way to the playful pleasure and athletic enthusiasm provoked by the sight of the chariot race, boxing, wrestling and archery contests, described in terms with which we are perfectly familiar through our own sporting competitions. Rohde has observed with great acuity, and on incontestable philological bases, that funeral games were a part of the cult of the dead, and that this implies an attribution of the dead person's real participation in the games. The games were played with a 'dead man', as card players still play today. It is well known that Bachofen, for his part, took things even further, stating: 'all games have a mortuary character. . . . The *meta* is always a tombstone . . . and it is to this religious significance that games owe their presence in the world of tombs, whether on wall frescoes (as at Corneto) or on sarcophagus reliefs'. So it is in tombs that we encounter the most ancient examples of that miniaturization which, in the preceding pages, has been shown to be a cipher of the toy. As Ariès writes:

Historians of the toy, and collectors of dolls and toy miniatures, have always had considerable difficulty in separating the doll, the child's toy, from all the other images and statuettes which the sites of excavations yield up in wellnigh industrial quantities and which more often than not had a religious significance: objects of a household or funerary cult . . .[8]

If toys are the signifiers of diachrony, by what right do they feature in that immutable world of synchrony, the domain of the tomb? But that is not all. Lévi-Strauss mentions the case of the adoption rites which the Fox Indians celebrate to substitute a living parent for a dead one, and thereby allow the final departure of the deceased's soul. These ceremonies are accompanied by games of skill and chance and sporting competitions between the population, divided for the occasion into two groups, *Kicko* and *Tokan*, representing the living and the dead. But – and this is the interesting part – these games have the peculiarity that their outcome is pre-established: if the dead person belongs to the *Tokan* group, it is the *Tokanagi* who win; if he or she belongs to the *Kicko* group, then the *Kickoagi* win instead. In other words, we have before us a game which is treated as a ritual and which, ruling out contingency, can certainly no longer serve to transform structures into events. One might also say that game and rite, toys and ritual objects, signifiers of diachrony and signifiers of synchrony, differentiated during life, are inverted, and merge in death.

But let us take a closer look at the meaning and function of funeral ceremonies. What we find is a system of beliefs replicated without great variations between diverse and far-flung cultures, which we can therefore treat as a fairly unitary whole. According to these beliefs, death's first result is to transform the dead person into a phantom (the Latin *larva*, the Green *eídōlon* and *phásma*, the Indian *pitr*, etc.) – that is, into a vague, threatening being who remains in the world of the living and returns to the familiar places of the departed one. The purpose of funeral rites – scholars are in agreement on this – is to guarantee the transformation of this unsettling, restless being into a friendly and powerful ancestor living in a separate world, with whom relationships are ritually defined. But if we try to specify the nature of this vague threatening 'larva', we see that all the evidence concurs: the ghost is the 'image' of the dead man, his likeness, a kind of shadow or mirror reflection (it is the image that appears to Achilles to ask him for burial, and the hero cannot overcome his amazement at the perfect resemblance to Patroclus: 'he bore a wondrous likeness', he exclaims).

We can then perhaps try to construct this complex of apparently disconcerting beliefs into a coherent system. Death transports the deceased from the sphere of the living – where diachronic and synchronic signifiers coexist – into that of the dead, where there is only synchrony. But in this process, diachrony, which has been evacuated, will invest the signifier *par excellence* of synchrony: the image, which death has separated from its corporeal support and set free. So the ghost is a signifier of synchrony which appears threateningly in the world of the living as an unstable signifier *par excellence*, which can assume the diachronic signified of a perpetual wandering (*alástōr*, the wanderer, is what the Greeks called the spectre of the unburied), and the impossibility of attaining a state of fixity. Yet it is this very signifier which, through its potential for semantic inversion, facilitates a bridge between the world of the living and that of the dead, ensuring the passage from the one to the other without, however, confusing the two. In this way, death (the gravest threat that nature brings to bear on the binary system of human society, for it is hardest to keep open the signifying opposition between diachrony and synchrony on which the system is founded once these seem to coincide) is overcome, thanks to one of those unstable signifiers whose function we have already learned to value in the *churinga* and the toy. The *larva*, the unstable signifier between synchrony and diachrony, is transformed into *lare*, the mask and graven image of the ancestor which, as a stable signifier, guarantees the continuity of the system. In the words of a Chinese proverb quoted by Granet: 'The soul-breath of the dead wanders: thus we make masks to give it a resting place.'[9]

It now becomes clear why this requires very special ceremonies which do not entirely fit into either the schema of ritual nor that of play, but seem to partake of both. Unlike other rites (and games), the object of funeral rites is not the conveying of stable signifiers from the sphere of diachrony into that of synchrony, or vice versa: their object is the transformation of unstable signifiers into stable signifiers. Thus games enter into funeral ceremonies, but in order to be treated as elements of a ritual; and while rites and games allow the survival of unstable signifiers, funeral ritual-games cannot leave residues: the ghost – an unstable signifier – must become the dead person, a stable signifier of synchrony.[10]

But the signifying opposition between synchrony and diachrony, between the world of the dead and the world of the living, is shattered not only by death. It is threatened by another critical moment, no less to be feared: birth. Thus here too we see unstable signifiers come into play: just as death does not immediately produce ancestors, but ghosts, so birth does not immediately produce men and women, but babies, which in all societies have a special differential status. If the ghost is the living-dead or the half-dead person, the baby is a dead-living or a half-alive person. It too, as tangible proof of the discontinuity between the world of the living and the world of the dead, and between diachrony and synchrony, and as an unstable signifier which can, at any moment, be transformed into its own opposite, thereby represents both a threat to be neutralized and a means of enabling the passage from one sphere to the other without abolishing its signifying difference. And just as ghosts have a corresponding function to that of children, so funeral rites correspond to initiation rites, in their purpose of transforming these unstable signifiers into stable signifiers.

From a starting point in Christmas folklore, with its central figure of Father Christmas, in just a few unforgettable pages Lévi-Strauss reconstructed the meaning of initiation rites;[11] behind the adult-child opposition, he discerned a more basic opposition between living and dead. In fact, as we have seen, children correspond less to the dead than to ghosts. Within the perspective of signifying function, adults and dead belong to the same order, that of stable signifiers and the continuity between diachrony and synchrony.

(From this point of view, there is little difference between cold societies, which represent this continuity as a circle in which the living become dead and these in turn become living, and hot societies like ours, which develop this continuity in a rectilinear process. In either case what matters is the continuity of the system.) But children and ghosts, as unstable signifiers, represent the discontinuity and difference between the two worlds. The dead person is not the ancestor: this is the meaning of the ghost. The ancestor is not the living man: this is the meaning of the child. For if the dead immediately became ancestors and ancestors immediately became living men, then the whole present would in an instant be transformed into past, and the whole past into present, and this would diminish that differential margin between synchrony and diachrony on which is based the potential for signifying relations, and with it the potential for human society and history. Thus, since ritual allows the persistence in the *churinga* of an irreducible diachronic residue, and play allows a synchronic residue in the toy, so the passage between the world of the living and the world of the dead allows the persistence of two points of discontinuity which are necessary to maintain the operation of a signifying function. So the passage between synchrony and diachrony, between world of the living and world of the dead, occurs in a kind of 'quantum leap', in which the unstable signifiers are the cipher:

Within this perspective, ghosts and children, belonging neither to the signifiers of diachrony nor to those of synchrony, appear as the signifiers of the same signifying opposition between the two worlds which constitutes the potential for a social system. *They are, therefore, the signifiers of the signifying function*, without which there would be neither human time nor history. Playland and the land of ghosts set out a utopian topology of historyland, which has no site except in a signifying difference between diachrony and synchrony, between *aiōn* and *chrónos*, between living and dead, between nature and culture.

So the social system can be pictured as a complex mechanism in which (unstable) signifiers of signification are counterposed to stable signifiers, but where in reality an exchange takes place between them to guarantee the functioning of the system. Thus adults submit to becoming ghosts so that the ghosts can become dead, and the dead become children so that the children can become men and women. The object of funeral rites and initiation rites, therefore, is the transmission of the signifying function, which must resist and endure beyond birth and death.[12] Thus no society, whether the hottest and most progressive or the coldest and most conservative, can altogether do without unstable signifiers and, in so far as they represent an element of disturbance and threat, must take care that the signifying exchange is not interrupted, so that phantoms can become dead and babies living men.

So if we now look at our own culture, which is convinced that it has freed itself from these problems and rationally resolved the transmission of signifiers from the past to the present, it will not take us long to recognize 'larve' in the *Nachleben* and in those survivors of the signifiers of the past, stripped of their original meaning, to which the Warburghian school has dedicated such fertile and exemplary studies. The frozen images of the pagan gods and the fearsome figures of the astrological decans and paranatellons, whose larval and larvate survival we can trace without a break across the centuries, like the rest of the innumerable signifiers of the past, shorn of their meaning, appear as oppressive and troubling symbols; these are the precise equivalent of the *larve*, these *are* the ghosts which cultures keep alive, in so far as they exorcize them as threatening phantoms, instead of playing with them.

As for the other class of unstable signifiers, a look at the function our society reserves for the young is no less instructive. For it is certainly not an index of health when a culture is so obsessed with the signifiers of its own past that it prefers to exorcize them and keep them alive indefinitely as 'phantoms' rather than bury them, and when it is so afraid of the unstable signifiers of the present that it cannot see them as anything other than the bearers of disorder and subversion. This exasperation and this hardening of the signifying function of ghosts and children in our culture is an unequivocal sign that the binary system has become blocked and can no longer guarantee the exchange of signifiers on which its functioning is founded. Hence those adults who use the ghosts of the past only as bogeys to prevent their own children from becoming adults, and use their own children only as an alibi for their own incapacity to bury the ghosts of the past, need to remember that the basic rule of the play of history is that the signifiers of continuity accept an exchange with those of discontinuity, and the transmission of the signifying function is more important than the signifiers themselves. True historical continuity cannot pretend to discard the signifiers of discontinuity by confining them to a Playland or a museum for ghosts (which now often coincide in a single place: the university), but by 'playing' with them, accepts them so as to restore them to the past and transmit them to the future. Otherwise, in the face of adults who literally play dead and prefer to entrust their own phantoms to children and children to these phantoms, the shades of the past will come back to life to devour the children, or the children will destroy the signifiers of the past – which, in terms of the signifying function, history, amounts to the same thing. This is the very opposite of the myth of origin narrated by one of the Pueblo Indians' initiation rites: when the shades of the dead came back to the world of the living to carry off the children, the adults offered to impersonate them every year in a playful masquerade, so that the children could live and one day take their place.

NOTES

1. C. Collodi, *The Adventures of Pinocchio*, transl. M.A. Murray, London: T. Fisher Unwin 1892.
2. M. Granet, *Danses et Légendes de la Chine ancienne*, Paris 1959, vol. I, p. 321.
3. C. Lévi-Strauss, 'Mythe et oubli', in *Langue, discours, société*, for Emile Benveniste, Paris 1975, p. 299.

4. E. Benveniste, 'Le jeu et le sacré', *Deucalion*, no. 2, 1947, p. 165.
5. ibid.
6. C. Lévi-Strauss, *La Pensée sauvage*, Paris: Plon 1962, pp. 44–7.
7. K. Kerényi, *Die Religion der Griechen und Römer*, Munich-Zürich 1963, p. 34.
8. Lévi-Strauss, *La Pensée sauvage*, p. 320.
9. P. Ariès, *Centuries of Childhood*, Harmondsworth 1973, p. 66.
10. Granet, *Danses et Légendes*, p. 335.
11. The case of the Trobriand islanders (studied by Malinowski in 'Baloma; the Spirits of the Dead in the Trobriand islands', in *Journal of the Royal Anthropological Institute of Great Britain and Ireland*, vol. 46, 1916) has a particular structure that fully confirms this interpretation. What is usually presented as a single unstable signifier here appears from the beginning divided into two distinct signifiers: the Baloma (the image, born into the land of the dead) and the Kosi (the shade, which wanders for some time in the neighbourhood of the village before disappearing without any need of special human intervention). In this case, too, the signifying opposition between diachrony and synchrony is thus guaranteed at the moment of death; but since the unstable signifier is already broken into two separate components, the funeral ceremonies, as Malinowski noted, do not appear to concern the spirit of the dead one in any way: 'They are not performed, either to send a message of love and regret to the *baloma* (spirit), or to deter him from returning; they do not influence his welfare, nor do they affect his relation to the survivors.'
12. C. Lévi-Strauss, 'Le Père Noël supplicié', *Les Temps Modernes*, no. 77, 1952.
13. An analysis of an initiation rite which has always greatly fascinated ethnographers, the *katcina* of the Pueblo Indians, is particularly instructive in this context. In the course of this initiation, the adults reveal no teaching or system of truths to the initiands, only that the *katcina*, the supernatural beings whom they have seen dance in the village in the course of annual ceremonies, and who have so often frightened them with their yucca whips, are the adults themselves *masked as katcina*. This revelation, however, commits the neophytes to keeping the secret and, in their turn, impersonating the *katcina*. The content of the ritual, the 'secret' which is transmitted is, in other words, that there is nothing to transmit *except transmission itself*: the signifying function in itself.

TIME AND HISTORY

Critique of the Instant and the Continuum

To Victor Goldschmidt and Henri-Charles Puech

I

Every conception of history is invariably accompanied by a certain experience of time which is implicit in it, conditions it, and thereby has to be elucidated. Similarly, every culture is first and foremost a particular experience of time, and no new culture is possible without an alteration in this experience. The original task of a genuine revolution, therefore, is never merely to 'change the world', but also – and above all – to 'change time'. Modern political thought has concentrated its attention on history, and has not elaborated a corresponding concept of time. Even historical materialism has until now neglected to elaborate a concept of time that compares with its concept of history. Because of this omission it has been unwittingly compelled to have recourse to a concept of time dominant in Western culture for centuries, and so to harbour, side by side, a revolutionary concept of history and a traditional experience of time. The vulgar representation of time as a precise and homogeneous continuum has thus diluted the Marxist concept of history: it has become the hidden breach through which ideology has crept into the citadel of historical materialism. Benjamin had already warned of this danger in his 'Theses on the Philosophy of History'. We now need to elucidate the concept of time implicit in the Marxist conception of history.

II

Since the human mind has the experience of time but not its representation, it necessarily pictures time by means of spatial images. The Graeco-Roman concept of time is basically circular and continuous. Puech writes:

> Dominated by a notion of intelligibility which assimilates the full, authentic being to what is in him and corresponds to him, to the eternal and the immutable, the Greek regards movement and becoming as inferior degrees of reality, where correspondence is at best only understood as permanence and perpetuity, in other words as return. Circular movement, which guarantees the unchanged preservation of things through their repetition and continual return, is the most direct and most perfect expression (and therefore the closest to the divine) of the zenith of the hierarchy: absolute immobility.

In Plato's *Timaeus* time is measured by the cyclical revolution of the celestial spheres and defined as a moving image of eternity: 'The creator of the world constructed a moving image of eternity, and, in ordering the heavens, from eternity one and unshifting he made this image which ever moves according to the laws of number and which we call time.' Aristotle confirms the circular nature of time in these terms:

> . . . and so time is regarded as the rotation of the sphere, inasmuch as all other orders of motion are measured by it, and time itself is standardized by reference to it. And this is the reason of our habitual way of speaking; for we say that human affairs and those of all other things that have natural movement . . . seem to be in a way circular, because all these things come to pass in time and have their beginning and end as it were 'periodically'; for time itself is conceived as coming round; and this again because time and such a standard rotation mutually

determine each other. Hence, to call the happenings of a thing a circle is saying that there is a sort of circle of time . . .[1]

The first outcome of this conception is that time, being essentially circular, has no direction. Strictly speaking, it has no beginning, no middle and no end – or rather, it has them only in so far as its circular motion returns unceasingly back on itself. A singular passage in Aristotle's *Problemata* explains that from this point of view it is impossible to say whether we are before or after the Trojan War:

> Do those who lived at the time of the Trojan War come before us, and before them those who lived in an even more ancient time, and so on to infinity, those men most remote in the past coming always before the rest? Or else, if it is true that the universe has a beginning, a middle and an end; that what in ageing reaches its end to find itself therefore back at the beginning; if it is true, on the other hand, that the things that are closest to the beginning come before, what then prevents us from being closer to the beginning than those who lived at the time of the Trojan War? . . . If the sequence of events forms a circle, since the circle has indeed neither beginning nor end, we cannot, by being closer to the beginning, come before them any more than they can be said to come before us.

But the fundamental character of the Greek experience of time – which, through Aristotle's *Physics*, has for two millennia determined the Western representation of time – is its being a precise, infinite, quantified continuum. Aristotle thus defines time as 'quantity of movement according to the before and the after', and its continuity is assured by its division into discrete instants [*to nyn*, the now], analogous to the geometric point [*stigmé*]. The instant in itself is nothing more than the continuity of time [*synécheia chrónou*], a pure limit which both joins and divides past and future. As such, it is always elusive, and Aristotle expresses its paradoxically nullified character in the statement that in dividing time infinitely, the now is always 'other'; yet in uniting past and future and ensuring continuity, it is always the same; and in this is the basis of the radical 'otherness' of time, and of its 'destructive' character:

> And besides, since the 'now' is the end and the beginning of time, but not of the same time, but the end of time past and the beginning of time to come, it must present a relation analogous to the kind of identity between the convexity and the concavity of the same circumference, which necessitates a difference between that with respect to which it bears the other.[2]

Western man's incapacity to master time, and his consequent obsession with gaining it and passing it, have their origins in this Greek concept of time as a quantified and infinite *continuum* of precise fleeting instants.

A culture with such a representation of time could have no real experience of historicity. To state that Antiquity had no experience of lived time is, without doubt, a simplification, but there is equally no doubt that the locus in which the Greek philosophers deal with the question of time is always *Physics*. Time is something objective and natural, which envelops things that are 'inside' it as if in a sheath [*periechón*]: as each thing inhabits a place, so it inhabits time. The beginning of the modern concept of history has often been traced back to the words with which Herodotus opens his *Histories*: 'Herodotus of Halicarnassus here puts forth the fruit of his researches, so that time may not erase men's undertakings . . .'. It is the destructive character of time which the *Histories* wish to combat, thereby confirming the essentially ahistorical nature of the ancient concept of time. Like the word indicating the act of knowledge [*eidénai*], so too the word *historia* derives from the root *id-*, which means to see. *Hístōr* is in origin the eyewitness, the one who has seen. Here too the Greek supremacy of vision is confirmed. The determination of authenticity as 'present before the look' rules out an experience of history as what is already there without ever appearing before our eyes as such.

III

The antithesis of this in many respects is the Christian experience of time. While the classical representation of time is a circle, the image guiding the Christian conceptualization of it is a straight line. Puech writes:

> In contrast with the Hellenic world, for the Christian the world is created within time and must end within time. At one end, the account of Genesis, at the other, the eschatological perspective of the Apocalypse. And the Creation, the Last Judgement, and the intermediary period between these two events are unique. This uniquely fashioned universe which began, which endures and which will end within time, is a finite world enclosed by the two edges of its history. Its duration comprises neither the eternal nor the infinite, and the events which unfold within it will never be repeated.

Moreover, in contrast with the directionless time of the classical world, this time has a direction and a purpose: it develops irreversibly from the Creation to the end, and has a central point of reference in the incarnation of Christ, which shapes its development as a progression from the initial fall to the final redemption. Thus Saint Augustine can oppose the *falsi circuli* of the Greek philosophers with the *via recta* of Christ, and the eternal repetition of paganism, where nothing is new, with Christian *novitas*, in which everything always occurs only once. The history of humanity thus appears as a history of salvation, the progressive realization of redemption, whose foundation is in God. And in this, every event is unique and irreplaceable.

Despite its apparent scorn for 'epoch', it is Christianity which has laid the foundation for an experience of historicity, rather than the ancient world, attentive though it was to events. Indeed, Christianity resolutely separates time from the natural movement of the stars to make it an essentially human, interior phenomenon. 'Supposing the lights of heaven were to cease,' writes Saint Augustine, in singularly modern-sounding phraseology,

> and the potter's wheel moved on, would there not be time by which we could measure its rotations and say that these were at equal intervals, or some slower, some quicker, some taking longer, some shorter? Let no one tell me that the movement of the heavenly bodies is time. . . . I see time as in some way extended. But do I see it? Or do I only seem to see it? Thou wilt show me, O Light, O Truth.[3]

None the less, time thus interiorized remains the continuous succession of precise instants of Greek thought. The whole of the eleventh book of Augustine's *Confessions*, with its anguished and unresolved interrogation of fleeting time, shows that continuous, quantified time has not been abolished, simply displaced from the paths of the stars to interior duration. Indeed, it is precisely his preservation of the Aristotelian concept of the precise instant which prevents Augustine from reaching a conclusion about the question of time:

> But the two times, past and future, how can they be, since the past is no more and the future is not yet? On the other hand, if the present were always present and never flowed away into the past, it would not be time at all, but eternity. But if the present is only time, because it flows away into the past, how can we say that it is? For it is, only because it will cease to be . . .
>
> If we conceive of some point of time which cannot be divided even into the minutest parts of moments, that is the only point that can be called present: and that point flees at such lightning speed from being future to being past, that it has no extent of duration at all. For if it were so extended, it would be divisible into past and future: the present has no length.[4]

The experience of a fuller, more original and tangible time, discernible in primitive Christianity, is thereby overlaid by the mathematical time of classical Antiquity. With it there inevitably returns the ancient circular representation of Greek metaphyiscs, assimilated first through Neoplatonizing patristics, and later through scholastic theology. Eternity, the regime of divinity, with its static circle, tends to negate the human experience of time. The discrete, fleeting instant becomes the point where time intercepts the wheel of eternity. 'To achieve an image of the relation between eternity and time,' we read in Guillaume d'Auvergne's *de Universo*:

> try to imagine eternity as an immense wheel, and within this wheel the wheel of time, so that the first touches the second at a single point. For you know that if a circle or a sphere touches another circle or another sphere, whether outside or inside, this contact can take place only at a single point. Since eternity is entirely motionless and simultaneous, as I have said, whenever the wheel of time touches the wheel of eternity the contact occurs only at a regular point in its rotation; this is why time is not simultaneous.[5]

IV

The modern concept of time is a secularization of rectilinear, irreversible Christian time, albeit sundered from any notion of end and emptied of any other meaning but that of a structured process in terms of before and after. This representation of time as homogeneous, rectilinear and empty derives from the experience of manufacturing work and is sanctioned by modern mechanics, which establishes the primacy of uniform rectilinear motion over circular motion. The experience of dead time abstracted from experience, which characterizes life in modern cities and factories, seems to give credence to the idea that the precise fleeting instant is the only human time. Before and after, notions which were vague and empty for Antiquity – and which, for Christianity, had meaning only in terms of the end of time – now become meaning in themselves and for themselves, and this meaning is presented as truly historical.

As Nietzsche had already grasped, with Hartmann's 'process of the world' ('only process can lead to redemption'), the idea governing the nineteenth-century concept of history is that of 'process'. Only process as a whole has meaning, never the precise fleeting *now*; but since this process is really no more than a simple succesion of *now* in terms of before and after, and the history of salvation has meanwhile become pure chronology, a semblance of meaning can be saved only by introducing the idea – albeit one lacking any rational foundation – of a continuous, infinite progress. Under the influence of the natural sciences, 'development' and 'progress', which merely translate the idea of a chronologically orientated process, become the guiding categories of historical knowledge. Such a concept of time and history necessarily expropriates man from the human dimension and impedes access to authentic historicity. As Dilthey and Count Yorck had observed ('That school was by no means a historical one, but an antiquarian one, construing things aesthetically, while the great dominating activity was one of mechanical construction'[6]), behind the apparent triumph of historicism in the nineteenth century is hidden a radical negation of history, in the name of an ideal of knowledge modelled on the natural sciences.

This leaves ample scope for the Lévi-Straussian critique, which points to the chronological and discontinuous nature of historiographical codification, and denounces fraudulent pretensions to any objective historical continuity independent of the code (with the result that history ultimately assumes the role of a 'thoroughgoing myth'). Lévi-Strauss rejects the equation of history and humanity, which is thrust upon us with the undeclared aim of 'making history the last refuge of transcendental humanism'.

But it is not a question of abandoning history; rather, of achieving a more authentic concept of historicity.

V

Hegel thinks of time in terms of the Aristotelian model of the precise instant. Against the Aristotelian *nyn*, he sets the *now* in correspondence; and, as Aristotle conceived the *nyn* as *stigmē*, so he conceives the *now* as a point. This now, which 'is nothing other than the passage of its being into nothingness, and from nothingness into its being', is eternity as 'true present'. The conjunction of spatial representations and temporal experience which dominates the Western concept of time is developed in Hegel as a conception of time as negation and dialectical dominion of space. While the spatial point is a simple indifferent negativity, the temporal point – that is, the instant – is the negation of this undifferentiated negation, the overcoming of the 'paralysed immobility' of space in becoming. It is therefore, in this sense, negation of negation.

Defining time in this way as a negation of negation, Hegel cannot avoid taking to its extreme conclusion the nullification of experience by time implicit in its determination as a continuous succession of precise instants. 'Time', he writes in a passage from the *Encyclopaedia* which still resonates with an – albeit subdued and consciously assumed – Augustinian anxiety in the face of time's fleeting essence, 'is the thing existing which is not when it is, and is when it is not: a half-glimpsed becoming.' As such, this negative being which 'is what is not and is not what is' is formally homologous to man. Indeed, perhaps it is because Hegel thinks of time in terms of the metaphysical model of the precise instant that it can form such a part in his system of that 'power of the negative', which he sees at work in the human spirit and makes the central motor of the dialectic. What the Hegelian system expresses in the formal correspondence of time and the human spirit, both of these construed as negation of negation, is the as yet unexplored link between the annulled experience of time for Western man and the negating power of his culture. Only a culture with such an experience of time could render the essence of the human spirit as negation, and the true sense of the Hegelian dialectic cannot be understood unless it is related to the concept of time to which it is integral. For the dialectic is above all what makes possible the containment and unification [*dia-légesthai*] of the continuum of negative fleeting instants.

Nevertheless, in Hegel the origin of time and the sense of its formal correspondence with the spirit are not interrogated as such. Time appears simply as the necessity and the destiny of the unfulfilled spirit. The spirit must *fall* into time. 'It is in keeping with the concept of the spirit', he writes in *Reason in History*, 'that the evolution of history be produced in time.' But since time, as we have seen, 'is the thing existing which is not when it is, and is when it is not', the Absolute can be true only as an 'outcome'; and history, which is 'the spirit alienated in time', is essentially *Stufengang*, a gradual process. As the alienation of alienation, it is the 'calvary' and the 'discovery' of the absolute spirit, the 'foam' which rises forth for him from the 'chalice' of his own infinitude.[7]

Like time, whose essence is pure negation, history can never be grasped in the instant, but only as total social process. It thereby remains at one remove from the lived experience of the single individual, whose ideal is happiness. 'In considering history one can also adopt the viewpoint of happiness, but history is not the site of happiness.' Hence the emergence, in the Hegelian philosophy of history, of the sombre figure of 'great historical individuality' in which is incarnated 'the soul of the world'. 'Great men' are merely instrumental in the forward march of the universal Spirit. Like individuals, 'they do not know what is commonly held as happiness'. 'Once they have reached their goal, they sag like empty sacks.' The real subject of history is the State.

VI

Marx's conception of history has an altogether different context. For him history is not something into which man *falls*, something that merely expresses the being-in-time of the human mind, it is man's original dimension as *Gattungswesen* (species-being), as being capable of generation – that is to say, capable of producing himself from the start not merely as an individual, nor as an abstract generalization, but as a universal individual. History, therefore, is determined not, as it is in Hegel and the historicism which derives from him, by an experience of linear time as negation of negation, but by *praxis*, concrete activity as essence and origin [*Gattung*] of man. *Praxis*, in which man posits himself as origin and nature of man, is at once 'the first historical act', the founding act of history, to be understood as the means by which the human essence becomes man's nature and nature becomes man. History is no longer, as in Hegel, man's destiny of alienation and his necessary fall within the negative time which he inhabits in an infinite process, but rather his *nature*; in other words, man's original belonging to himself as *Gattungswesen*, from which alienation has temporarily removed him. *Man is not a historical being because he falls into time, but precisely the opposite; it is only because he is a historical being that he can fall into time, temporalizing himself.*

Marx did not elaborate a theory of time adequate to his idea of history, but the latter clearly cannot be reconciled with the Aristotelian and Hegelian concept of time as a continuous and infinite succession of precise instants. So long as this nullified experience of time remains our horizon, it is not possible to attain authentic history, for truth will always vie with the process as a whole, and man will never be able concretely, practically, to appropriate his own history. The fundamental contradiction of modern man is precisely that he does not yet have an experience of time adequate to his idea of history, and is therefore painfully split between his being-in-time as an elusive flow of instants and his being-in-history, understood as the original dimension of man. The twofold nature of every modern concept of history, as *res gestae* and as *historia rerum gestarum*, as diachronic reality and as synchronic structure which can never coincide in time, expresses this impossibility: the inability of man, who is lost in time, to take possession of his own historical nature.

VII

Whether it is conceived as linear or circular, in Western thought time invariably has the point as its dominating feature. Lived time is represented through a metaphysical-geometric concept (the discrete point or instant), and it is then taken as if this concept were itself the real time of experience. Vico had observed that the concept of the geometric point is a metaphysical concept, which furnished the *malignum aditum*, the 'evil opening' through which metaphysics had invaded physics. Vico's words on the geometric point could also be applied to the instant as a 'point' in time. This is the opening through which the eternity of metaphysics insinuates itself into the human experience of time, and irreparably splits it. Any attempt to conceive of time differently must inevitably come into conflict with this concept, and a critique of the instant is the logical condition for a new experience of time.

The elements for a different concept of time lie scattered among the folds and shadows of the Western cultural tradition. We need only to elucidate these, so that they may emerge as the bearers of a message which is meant for us and which it is our task to verify. It is in Gnosticism, that failed religion of the West, that there appears an experience of time in radical opposition to both the Greek and the Christian versions. In opposition to the Greek circle of experience and the straight line of Christianity, it posits a concept whose spatial model can be represented by a broken line. In this way it strikes directly at what remains unaltered in classical Antiquity and Christianity alike: duration, precise and continuous time. The cosmic time of Greek experience is denied by Gnosticism in the name of the world's absolute estrangement from a god (God is the *allótrios*, the supreme other), whose providential work cannot be a matter of preserving cosmic laws, but of breaking them. The impetus towards redemption of Christian linear time is negated because, for the Gnostic, the Resurrection is not something to be awaited in time, to occur in some more or less remote future; it has already taken place.

The time of Gnosticism, therefore, is an incoherent and unhomogeneous time, whose truth is in the moment of abrupt interruption, when man, in a sudden act of consciousness, takes possession of his own condition of being resurrected ('statim resurrectionis compos'). In keeping with this experience of interrupted time, the Gnostic attitude is resolutely revolutionary: it refuses the past while valuing in it, through an exemplary sense of the present, precisely what was condemned as negative (Cain, Esau, the inhabitants of Sodom), and expecting nothing from the future.

In Stoicism, too, the twilight of Antiquity seems to overcome its own concept of time. This appears as a refusal of the astronomical time of the *Timaeus*, image of eternity, and of the Aristotelian notion of the mathematical instant. For the Stoics, homogeneous, infinite, quantified time, dividing the present into discrete instants, is unreal time, which exemplifies experience as waiting and deferral. Subservience to this elusive time constitutes a fundamental sickness, which, with its infinite postponement, hinders human existence from taking possession of itself as something full and singular ('maximum vitae vitium est, quod imperfecta semper est, quod ali quid in illa differtur'). Against this, the Stoic posits the liberating experience of time as something neither objective nor removed from our control, but springing from the actions and decisions of man. Its model is the *cairós*, the abrupt and sudden conjunction where decision grasps opportunity and life is fulfilled in the moment. Infinite, quantified time is thus at once delimited and made present: within itself the *cairós* distils different times ('omnium temporum in unum collatio') and within it the sage is master of himself and at his ease, like a god in eternity. This is 'the final hand' dealt every time to life, which radically removes man from servitude to quantified time ('qui cotidie vitae suae summam manum imposuit, non indiget tempore').

VIII

It is certainly no accident that every time modern thought has come to reconceptualize time, it has inevitably had to begin with a critique of continuous, quantified time. Such a critique underlies both Benjamin's 'Theses on the Philosophy of History' and Heidegger's incomplete analysis of temporality in *Being and Time*. This coincidence in two thinkers so far apart is a sign that the concept of time which has dominated Western culture for nearly two thousand years is on the wane.

There moves in Benjamin that same Jewish messianic intuition which had led Kafka to write that 'the Day of Judgement is the normal condition of history' and to replace the idea of history developing along infinite linear time with the paradoxical image of a 'state of history', whose key event is always unfolding and whose goal is not in the distant future, but already present. Taking up these themes, Benjamin seeks a concept of history corresponding to the statement that 'the state of emergency is the rule'. Instead of the nullified present of the metaphysical tradition, Benjamin posits 'a present which is not a transition, but in which time stands still and has come to a stop'. Instead of the social democratic and historicist notion of the historical progress of humankind, which 'cannot be sundered from the concept of its progression through a homogeneous, empty time', he puts forward the revolutionaries' 'awareness that they are about to make the continuum of history explode'. Against the empty, quantified instant, he sets a 'time of the now', *Jetzt-Zeit*, construed as a messianic cessation of happening, which 'comprises the entire history of mankind in an enormous abridgement'. It is in the name of this 'full time', which is 'the true site of historical construction', that Benjamin, faced with the Nazi-Soviet pact, pursues his lucid critique of the causes behind the European Left's disastrous failure after the First World War. The messianic time of Judaism, in which every second was the 'strait gate through which the Messiah might enter', thus becomes the model for a conception of history 'that avoids any complicity with the thinking to which politicians continue to adhere'.[8]

But it is in Heidegger's thought that the conception of precise, continuous time is subjected to a radical critique within the terms of repetition–destruction which invade Western metaphysics as a whole. From the start, Heidegger's research was directed towards a siting of history that would overcome vulgar historicism, and in which, 'with the thesis that "*Dasein* is historical", one has in view not just the Ontical Fact that in man we are presented with a more or less important "atom in the workings of world history . . ."'[9] Thus, at the very point when they were seen to be inadequate, he took up Dilthey's efforts towards a historical foundation for the human sciences independent of the natural sciences. But the originality of *Sein und Zeit* is that the foundation of historicity takes place in tandem with an analysis of temporality which elucidates a different and more authentic experience of time. At the heart of this experience there is no longer the precise, fleeting *instant* throughout linear time, but the *moment* of the authentic decision in which the *Dasein* experiences its own finiteness, which at every moment extends from birth to death ('A *Dasein* which no longer exists . . . is not past, in the ontologically strict sense; it is rather *having-been-there*'),[10] and, throwing itself forward in care, it freely assumes the destiny of its primordial historicity. Man does not fall into time, 'but exists as primordial temporalization'. Only because he is in his being both anticipatory and having-been can he assume his own thrownness and be, in the moment 'of his own time'.

It would be easy to show how this foundation of historicity as care in the being of man is in no way opposed to the Marxist foundation of historicity in praxis, albeit in a different area, with both located as polar opposites to vulgar historicism. Thus Heidegger, in his *Letters on Humanism*, was able to write that 'the Marxist concept of history is superior to any other historiography'. It is perhaps more interesting to note that in his later writing, when *Sein und Zeit*'s project of conceptualizing time as the framework for understanding being was abandoned, Heidegger's thought is focused on how, given that metaphysics had now been overtaken, human historicity could be conceived in a totally new way. This is not the place to attempt an explanation of the concept of *Ereignis* (Event), which designates both the centre and the extreme limit of Heidegger's thought after *Sein und Zeit*. From the perspective which interests us here we must, however, at least acknowledge that it allows the Event to be conceived no longer as a spatio-temporal determination but as the opening of the primary *dimension* in which all spatio–temporal dimensions are based.

IX

Yet for everyone there is an immediate and available experience on which a new concept of time could be founded. This is an experience so essential to human beings that an ancient Western myth makes it humankind's original home: it is pleasure. Aristotle had realized that pleasure was a heterogeneous thing in relation to the experience of quantified, continuous time. 'The from [*eîdos*] of pleasure' – he writes in the *Nicomachean Ethics* – is perfect [*teleion*] at any moment', adding that pleasure, unlike movement, does not occur in a space of time, but is 'within each now something whole and complete'. This lack of correspondence between pleasure and quantified time, which we seem to have forgotten, was so familiar in the Middle Ages that Aquinas could answer in the negative to the question 'utrum delectatio sit in tempore'; and it was this same awareness which upheld the Provençal troubadours' Edenic project of a perfect pleasure [*fin'amors, joi*] outside any measurable duration.

This does not mean that pleasure has its place in eternity. The Western experience of time is split between eternity and continuous linear time. The dividing point through which the two relate is the instant as a discrete, elusive point. Against this conception, which dooms any attempt to master time, there must be opposed one whereby the true site of pleasure, as man's primary dimension, is neither precise, continuous time nor eternity, but history. Contrary to what Hegel stated, it is only as the source and site of happiness that history can have a meaning for man. In this sense, Adam's seven hours in Paradise are the primary core of all authentic historical experience. For history is not, as the dominant ideology would have it, man's servitude to continuous linear time, but man's liberation from it: the time of history and the *cairós* in which man, by his initiative, grasps favourable opportunity and chooses his own freedom in the moment. Just as the full, discontinuous, finite and complete time of pleasure must be set against the empty, continuous and infinite time of vulgar historicism, so the chronological time of pseudo-history must be opposed by the cairological time of authentic history.

True historical materialism does not pursue an empty mirage of continuous progress along infinite linear time, but is ready at any moment to stop time, because it holds the memory that man's original home is pleasure. It is this time which is experienced in authentic revolutions, which, as Benjamin remembers, have always been lived as a halting of time and an interruption of chronology. But a revolution from which there springs not a new chronology, but a qualitative alteration of time (a *cairology*), would have the weightiest consequence and would alone be immune to absorption into the reflux of restoration. He who, in the *epoché* of pleasure, has remembered history as he would remember his original home, will bring this memory to everything, will exact this promise from each instant: he is the true revolutionary and the true seer, released from time not at the millennium, but *now*.

NOTES

1. Aristotle, *Physics*, IV, XIV, transl. Philip H. Wickstead and Francis Cornford, London: Heinemann 1929.
2. ibid., IV, XIII.
3. Saint Augustine, *The Confessions*, Book Eleven, XXIII, transl. F.J. Sheed, London: Sheed & Ward 1944.

4. ibid., XIV.
5. Guillaume d'Auvergne, *De Universo*, in *Magistrum divinale*, Orléans 1674.
6. In M. Heidegger, *Being and Time*, transl. John Macquarrie and Edward Robinson, Oxford: Basil Blackwell 1967, p. 452.
7. Hegel, *Phenomenology of Spirit*, transl. A.V. Miller, Oxford: Clarendon Press 1977, p. 493.
8. W. Benjamin, 'Theses on the Philosophy of History', in *Illuminations*, transl. Harry Zohn, Glasgow: Fontana 1973.
9. Heidegger, p. 433.
10. Heidegger, p. 432.

THE PRINCE AND THE FROG

The Question of Method in Adorno and Benjamin

Theodor W. Adorno to Walter Benjamin

New York, 10 November 1938
Dear Walter:

The tardiness of this letter levels a menacing charge against me and all of us. But perhaps this accusation already contains a grain of defence. For it is almost self-evident that a full month's delay in my response to your Baudelaire cannot be due to negligence.

The reasons are entirely objective in nature. They involve the attitude of all of us to the manuscript, and, considering my special interest in the question of the *Arcades* study, I can probably say without immodesty, my attitude in particular. I had been looking forward to the arrival of the Baudelaire with the greatest eagerness and literally devoured it. I am full of admiration for the fact that you were able to complete it by the appointed time, and it is this admiration which makes it particularly hard for me to speak of what has come between my passionate expectation and the text itself.

Your idea of providing in the *Baudelaire* a model for the *Arcades* study was something I took very seriously, and I approached the satanic scene much as Faust approached the phantasmagoria of the Brocken mountain when he thought that many a riddle would now be solved. May I be excused for having had to give myself Mephistopheles' reply that many a riddle poses itself anew? Can you understand that reading your treatise, one of whose chapters is entitled *The Flâneur* and another *Modernism*, produced a certain disappointment in me?

The basic reason for this disappointment is that those parts of the study with which I am familiar do not constitute a model for the *Arcades* project so much as a prelude to it. Motifs are assembled but not elaborated. In your covering letter to Max [Horkheimer] you represented this as your express intention, and I am aware of the ascetic discipline which you impose on yourself to omit everywhere the conclusive theoretical answers to questions, and even make the questions themselves apparent only to initiates. But I wonder whether such an asceticism can be sustained in the face of such a subject and in a context which makes such powerful inner demands. As a faithful reader of your writings I know very well that in your work there is no lack of precedents for your procedure. I remember, for example, your essays on Proust and on Surrealism which appeared in *Die literarische Welt*. But can this method be applied to the complex of the *Arcades*? Panorama and 'traces', *flâneur* and arcades, modernism and the unchanging, *without* a theoretical interpretation – is this a 'material' which can patiently await interpretation without being consumed by its own aura? Rather, if the pragmatic content of these topics is isolated, does it not conspire in almost demonic fashion against the possibility of its own interpretation? In one of our unforgettable conversations in Königstein, you said that each idea in the *Arcades* had to be wrested away from a realm in which madness reigns. I wonder whether such ideas need to be as immured behind impenetrable layers of material as your ascetic discipline demands. In your present study the arcades are introduced with a reference to the narrowness of the pavements which impede the *flâneur* on the streets. This pragmatic introduction, it seems to me, prejudices the objectivity of phantasmagoria – something that I so stubbornly insisted upon even at the time of our Hornberg correspondence – as much as does the disposition of the first chapter to reduce phantasmagoria to types of behaviour of the literary *bohème.* You need not fear that I shall suggest that in your study phantasmagoria should survive unmediated or that the study itself should assume a phantasmagoric character. But the liquidation of phantasmagoria can only be accomplished with true profundity if they are treated as an objective historico-philosophical category and not as a 'vision' of social characters. It is precisely at this point that your conception differs from all other approaches to the 19th century. But the redemption of your postulate cannot be postponed for ever, or 'prepared' by a more harmless presentation of the matters in question. This is my objection. If in the third part, to use the old formulation, prehistory *in* the 19th century takes the place of the prehistory *of* the 19th century – most clearly in Péguy's statement about Victor Hugo – this is only another way of stating the same point.

But it seems to me that my objection by no means concerns only the questionable procedure of 'abstention' in a subject which is transported by ascetic refusal of interpretation towards a realm to which asceticism is opposed: the realm where history and magic oscillate. Rather, I see a close connection between the points at which your essay falls behind its own *a priori*, and its relationship to dialectical materialism – and here in particular I speak not only for myself but equally for Max, with whom I have had an exhaustive discussion of this question. Let me express myself in as simple and Hegelian a manner as possible. Unless I am very much mistaken, your dialectic lacks one thing: mediation. Throughout your text there is a tendency to relate the pragmatic contents of Baudelaire's work directly to adjacent features in the social history of his time, preferably economic features. I have in mind the passage about the duty on wine, certain statements about the barricades, or the above-mentioned passage about the arcades, which I find particularly problematic, for this is where the transition from a general theoretical discussion of physiologies to the 'concrete' representation of the *flâneur* is especially precarious.

I feel this artificiality wherever you put things in metaphorical rather than categorical terms. A case in point is the passage about the transformation of the city into an *intérieur* for the *flâneur*, where one of the most powerful ideas in your study seems to me to be presented as a mere as-if. There is a very close connection between such materialistic excursions, in which one never quite loses the apprehension that one feels for a swimmer who, covered with goose pimples, plunges into cold water, and the appeal to concrete modes of behaviour like that of the *flâneur*, or the subsequent passage about the relationship between seeing and hearing in the city, which not entirely by accident uses a quotation from Simmel. I am not entirely happy with all this. You need not fear that I shall take this opportunity to mount my hobby-horse. I shall content myself with serving it, in passing, a lump of sugar, and for the rest I shall try to give you the theoretical grounds for my aversion to that particular type of concreteness and its behaviouristic overtones. The reason is that I regard it as methodologically unfortunate to give conspicuous individual features from the realm of the superstructure a 'materialistic' turn by relating them immediately and perhaps even causally to corresponding features of the infrastructure. Materialist determination of cultural traits is only possible if it is mediated through the *total social process.*

Even though Baudelaire's wine poems may have been motivated by the wine duty and the town gates, the recurrence of these motifs in his work can only be explained by the overall social and economic tendency of the age – that is, in keeping with your formulation of the problem *sensu strictissimo*, by analysis of the commodity form in Baudelaire's epoch. No one is more familiar with the difficulties this involves than I am; the phantasmagoria chapter in my Wagner certainly has not settled these problems as yet. Your *Arcades* study in its definitive form will not be able to shirk the same obligation. The direct inference from the duty on wine to *L'Ame du Vin* imputes to phenomena precisely that kind of spontaneity, palpability and density which they have lost in capitalism. In this sort of immediate – I would almost say again, anthropological – materialism, there is a profoundly romantic element, and the more crassly and roughly you confront the Baudelairean world of forms with the necessities of life, the more clearly I detect it. The 'mediation' which I miss, and find obscured by materialistic-historiographic invocation, is nothing other than the theory which your study omits. The omission of the theory affects your empirical evidence itself. On the one hand, it lends it a deceptively epic character, and on the other it deprives the phenomena, which are experienced only subjectively, of their real historico-philosophical weight. To express it another way: the theological motif of calling things by their names tends to turn into a wide-eyed presentation of mere facts. If one wished to put it very drastically, one could say that your study is located at the crossroads of magic and positivism. That spot is bewitched. Only theory could break the spell – your own resolute, salutarily speculative theory. It is the claim of this theory alone that I am bringing against you . . .

This, I think, brings me to the centre of my criticism. The impression which your entire study conveys – and not only on me and my arcades orthodoxy – is that you have done violence to yourself. Your solidarity with the Institute [of Social Research], which pleases no one more than myself, has induced you to pay tributes to Marxism which are not really suited either to Marxism or to yourself. They are not suited to Marxism because the mediation through the total social process is missing, and you superstitiously attribute to material enumeration a power of illumination which is never kept for a pragmatic reference but only for theoretical construction. They do not suit your own individual nature because you have denied yourself your boldest and most fruitful ideas in a kind of pre-censorship according to materialist categories (which by no means coincide with the Marxist categories), even though it may be merely in the form of the above-mentioned postponement. I speak not only for myself, who am not qualified, but equally for Horkheimer and the others when I tell you that all of us are convinced that it would not only be beneficial to 'your' production if you elaborated your ideas without such considerations (in San Remo you raised counter-objections to this objection, and I am taking these very seriously), but that it would also be most helpful to the cause of dialectical materialism and the theoretical interests represented by the Institute, if you surrendered to your specific insights and conclusions without adding to them ingredients which you obviously find so distasteful to swallow that I cannot really regard them as beneficial. God knows, there is only one truth, and if your intelligence lays hold of this one truth in categories which on the basis of your idea of materialism may seem apocryphal to you, you will capture more of this one truth than if you use intellectual tools whose movements your hand resists at every turn . . .

Walter Benjamin's reply to Theodor W. Adorno

Paris, 9 December 1938

Dear Teddie:

It will not have surprised you to notice that it took me some time to draft my reply to your letter of 10 November. Even though the long delay in your letter made me suspect what it would say, it still came as a jolt to me. Also, I wanted to await the arrival of the galleys which you had promised me, and they did not come until 6 December. The time thus gained gave me a chance to weigh your critique as prudently as I could. I am far from considering it unfruitful, let alone incomprehensible. I will try to react to it in basic terms. . . .

Remembering our conversations in San Remo, I should like to proceed to the passage in your letter where you refer to them yourself. If I refused there, in the name of my own productive interests, to adopt an esoteric intellectual development for myself and, disregarding the interests of dialectical materialism, . . . to get down to business, this involved, in the final analysis, not . . . mere loyalty to dialectical materialism, but solidarity with the experiences which all of us have shared in the past 15 years. Here too, then, it is a matter of very personal productive interests of mine; I cannot deny that they may occasionally tend to do violence to my original interests. Between them lies an antagonism of which I would not even in my dreams wish to be relieved. The overcoming of this antagonism constitutes the problem of my study, and the problem is one of construction. I believe that speculation can start its necessarily bold flight with some prospect of success only if, instead of putting on the waxen wings of the esoteric, it seeks its source of strength in construction alone. It is because of the needs of construction that the second part of my book consists primarily of philo-logical material. What is involved there is less an 'ascetic discipline' than a methodological precaution. Incidentally, this philological part was the only one that could be completed independently – a circumstance which I had to bear in mind.

When you speak of a 'wide-eyed presentation of mere facts', you characterize the true philological attitude. This attitude was necessary not only for its results, but had to be built into the construction for its own sake. It is true that the indifference between magic and positivism, as you so aptly formulate it, should be liquidated. In other words, the philological inter-pretation of the author ought to be preserved and surpassed in the Hegelian manner by dialectical materialists. Philology is the examination of a text which proceeds by details and so magically fixates the reader on it. That which Faust took home in black and white,* and Grimm's devotion to little things, are closely related. They have in common that magical element whose exorcism is reserved for philosophy, here for the final part.

Astonishment, so you write in your *Kierkegaard*, indicates 'the profoundest insight into the relationship between dialectics, myth, and image'. It might be tempting for me to invoke this passage. But instead I propose to emend it (as I am planning to do on another occasion with a subsequent definition of the dialectical image). I believe it should say that astonishment is an outstanding *object* of such an insight. The appearance of closed facticity which attaches to a philological investigation and places the investigator under its spell, fades to the extent that the object is construed in an historical perspective. The base lines of this construction converge in our own historical experience. Thus the object constitutes itself as a monad. In the monad everything that used to lie in mythical rigidity as a textual reference comes alive. Therefore it seems a misjudgement of the matter to me if you find in my study a 'direct inference from the wine duty to *L'Ame du Vin*'. Rather, the juncture was established legitimately in the philological context – just as it would have been done in the interpretation of a classical writer. It gives to the poem the specific gravity which it assumes when it is properly read – something that has so far not been practised widely in the case of Baudelaire. Only when this poem has thus come into its own can the work be touched, or perhaps even shaken, by interpretation. For the poem in question, an interpretation would focus not on matters of taxation but on the significance of intoxication for Baudelaire.

If you think of other writings of mine, you will find that a critique of the attitude of the philologist is an old concern of mine, and it is basically identical with my critique of myth. Yet in each case it is this critique that provokes the philological effort itself. To use the language of *Elective Affinities*, it presses for the exhibition of the material content in which the truth content can be historically revealed. I can understand that this aspect of the matter was less to the fore in your mind. But so, therefore, were a number of important interpretations. I am thinking not only of interpretations of poems – *A une passante* – or of prose pieces – *The Man of the Crowd* – but above all of the unlocking of the concept of modernity, which it was my particular concern to keep within philological bounds. . . .

These two letters,[1] from which we have extracted the passages most closely touching on the problem of method, refer to the essay *The Paris of the Second Empire in Baudelaire*.[2] As part of his collaboration with the Institute of Social Research, Benjamin had sent this essay to Horkheimer and Adorno, who headed the Institute, in autumn 1938. The essay was conceived as part of the *Arcades* project, on which Benjamin worked, without achieving its completion, from 1927 until his death; it was, in Benjamin's words, intended to provide a 'model in miniature' for the *Arcades* project.

At first sight, Adorno's objections to the work seem correct. They stem from methodological reservations so deep and stubborn that he could still express them in almost identical terms in the early 1950s, by which time 'the name of the philosopher who took his life while fleeing Hitler's executioners' had acquired 'a certain nimbus'.[3] Adorno's description of Benjamin in *Prisms* tells us:

> his micrological and fragmentary method never entirely integrated the idea of universal mediation, which in Hegel as in Marx produces the totality. He never wavered in his fundamental conviction that the smallest cell of observed reality offset the rest of the world. To interpret phenomena materialistically meant for him not so much to elucidate them as products of the social whole but rather to relate them directly, in their isolated singularity, to material tendencies and social struggles.[4]

These objections are based on an interpretation of Marxist thought and, specifically, of the relationship between structure and superstructure, which lays claim to an enshrined orthodoxy, a belief in which leads every deviation from this relationship to be instantly dismissed as 'vulgar materialism'. Within these terms, Benjamin's analysis of Baudelaire's poetry is presented as a 'direct inference from the duty on wine to *L'Ame du vin*' – that is, as a direct imputing of causal relation between isolated features of the superstructure and corresponding features of the structure, leaving the impression of a tribute paid to Marxism which avails neither Marxism nor the author. Not the former 'because the mediation through the total social process is missing, and you superstitiously attribute to material enumeration a power of illumination which is never kept for a pragmatic reference but only for theoretical construction'. What flaws the work throughout is 'mediation. Throughout your text there is the tendency to relate the pragmatic contents of Baudelaire's work directly to adjacent features in the social history of his time.'

The accusation of 'vulgar materialism' could hardly be more explicitly expressed. From Adorno's doctrinal point of view, however, his argument seems perfectly coherent. Was it not Engels himself who, in a much-quoted letter to J. Bloch, stated that only *in the final instance* is production the determining historical factor? The yawning gap between structure and superstructure opened by this 'in the final instance' is bridged by Adorno through the appeal to 'mediation' and the 'total social process', thanks to which 'good' speculative theory is forearmed against any 'direct inference'. This 'universal mediation, which in both Hegel and Marx establishes totality', is the unassailable guarantee of Marxist orthodoxy in Adorno's critique, whereby his own doctrinal solidity is confirmed.

There remains only the regret that this critique is directed at a text which, as anyone who has read the essay in question will know, is perhaps the most illuminating analysis of a global cultural moment in the historical development of capitalism. To this regret is added a sense of unease, deriving from the fact that a critique founded on such incontrovertible doctrinal bases should have felt the need to borrow terminology that would seem more appropriate to the technical vocabulary of exorcism and ecclesiastical anathema than to a lucid philosophical refutation. Adorno has approached his friend's text like Faust at the 'satanic scene' of the phantasmagoria on the Brocken Mountain. Benjamin is accused of allowing the pragmatic content of his topics to conspire 'in almost demonic fashion' against the possibility of its own interpretation, and of having obscured mediation by 'materialist-historiographic invocation'. This language reaches its culmination in the passage where Benjamin's method is described in terms of a spell: 'If one wished to put it very drastically, one could say that your study is located at the crossroads of magic and positivism. That spot is bewitched. Only theory could break the spell. . . .'.

If it is true that every exorcism betrays its own solidarity with the exorcized one, it may be legitimate to advance some doubts about the theoretical foundation for Adorno's critique. Perhaps the superstitious 'power of illumination' whose exorcism is being sought is the very one being duly vindicated by the theory. And because the role of the exorcist is enacted here by 'mediation', perhaps it is worthwhile inspecting more closely the dialectical rationale on which it depends.

What Adorno is referring to by the term 'mediation' is clarified by his words: 'Materialist determination of cultural traits is only possible if it is mediated through the *total social process.*' These words, like the avowal that precedes them – 'let me express myself in as simple and Hegelian a manner as possible' – show that the mediation which Adorno has in mind is the one that is the object of Hegel's eulogy in a passage from the introduction to *Phenomenology of Spirit*, which it is appropriate to quote in its entirety:

The True is the whole. But the whole is nothing other than the essence consummating itself through its development. Of the Absolute it must be said that it is essentially a *result*, that only in the *end* is it what it truly is; and that precisely in this consists its nature, viz. to be actual, subject, the spontaneous becoming of itself. Though it may seem contradictory that the Absolute should be conceived essentially as a result, it needs little pondering to set this show of contradiction in its true light. The beginning, the principle, or the Absolute, as at first immediately enunciated, is only the universal. Just as when I say '*all* animals', this expression cannot pass for a zoology, so it is equally plain that the words, 'the Divine', 'the Absolute', 'the Eternal', etc., do not express what is contained in them; and only such words, in fact, do express the intuition as something immediate. Whatever is more than such a word, even the transition to a mere proposition, contains a *becoming-other* that has to be taken back, or is a mediation. But it is just this that is rejected with horror, as if absolute cognition were being surrendered when more is made of mediation than in simply saying that it is nothing absolute, and is completely absent in the Absolute.

But this abhorrence in fact stems from ignorance of the nature of mediation, and of absolute cognition itself. For mediation is nothing beyond self-moving selfsameness, or is reflection into self, the moment of the 'I' which is for itself pure negativity or, when reduced to its pure abstraction, *simple becoming.*[5]

The mediator interposing its good offices between structure and superstructure to safeguard materialism from vulgarity, therefore, is Hegelian dialectical historicism, which, like all go-betweens, is prompt in demanding its percentage. This percentage takes the form of renouncing the concrete grasp of each single event and each present instant of praxis in favour of deferral to the final instance of the total social process. Since the absolute is 'consequence', and 'only in the end is there truth', each single concrete moment of the process is real only as 'pure negativity' which the magic wand of dialectical mediation will transform – in the end – into the positive. There is but a short step from this to declaring that every moment in history is merely a means to an end, and the progressive historicism which dominates nineteenth-century ideology does it in a leap. Smuggling in this Hegelian concept of 'mediation' and 'total social process' as authentic Marxism means nothing less than erasing, at a stroke, the Marxist critique of Hegelian dialectic as 'abstract, formal process' which constitutes the melodic theme on which there unfolds the counterpoint of the 1844 Manuscript. Why, then, does Adorno – who is certainly not unaware of this critique – call upon mediation 'through the total social process' precisely to interpret the relationship between structure and superstructure, which Marx nowhere constructs as a dialectical relationship? The reason is, once again, to be found in the wish to be forearmed against a danger which, perhaps, he had ample reason to fear. Precisely because Marx does not present the relationship between material base and superstructure as a dialectical one, and seems instead to conceive it as a relationship of causal determination, it is necessary to call upon a mediator as a safeguard against the possibility of a 'vulgar' interpretation. But since the fear of vulgarity betrays the vulgarity of fear, so the suspicion of a vulgar interpretation is a suspicion whose formulator has reason to nurture most of all about himself. It is a fear of this kind which inspired in Engels his famous theory of the 'final instance' which is, it must be admitted, a masterpiece of hypocrisy. He warns against vulgar materialism by stating:

> According to the materialist conception of history, the *ultimately* determining element in history is the production and reproduction of real life. More than this neither Marx nor I have ever asserted. Hence if somebody twists this into saying that the economic element is the only determining one, he transforms that proposition into a meaningless, abstract, senseless phrase.[6]

But it is clear that if there was indeed distortion, it had already happened at the point when the relationship between material base and superstructure was interpreted as a relationship of cause and effect. Once this distortion took place, the only way to save it from its own vulgarity was to wave the bogey of vulgar materialism in one hand while the other hand got ready to do battle against it.

It is time to speak out and say that this bogey, like all bogeys, exists most of all within those who conjure it up. If Marx is not concerned to specify the way in which the relationship between structure and superstructure is to be construed, and has no fear of being occasionally considered 'vulgar', it is because an interpreatation of this relationship in a causal sense is not even conceivable in Marxist terms – a fact which renders superfluous the dialectical interpretation intended to remedy this. All causal interpretations are in fact consistent with Western metaphysics, and presuppose the sundering of reality into two different ontological levels. A materialism which conceived of economic factors as *causa prima*, in the same sense in which the God of metaphysics is *causa sui* and first principle of everything, would only be the obverse of metaphysics, not its rout. A similar ontological splitting irremediably betrays the Marxist concept of praxis as a concrete and unitary source reality, and it is this, rather than an alleged 'dialectical conception of cause and effect', which should be set against the vulgar interpretation. Praxis is not, in fact, something which needs a dialectical mediation in order to be represented as positive in the form of the superstructure, but is from the beginning 'what truly is', and from the beginning possesses wholeness and concreteness. If man finds his humanity in praxis, this is not because, in addition to carrying out productive work, he also transposes and develops these activities within a superstructure (by thinking, writing poetry, etc.); if man is human – if he is a *Gattungswesen*, a being whose essence is generic – his humanity and his species-being must be integrally present within the way in which he produces his material life – that is, within praxis. Marx abolishes the metaphysical distinction between *animal* and *ratio*, between nature and culture, between matter and form, in order to state that within praxis animality is humanity, nature is culture, matter is form. If this is true, the relationship between structure and superstructure can neither be one of causal determination nor one of dialectical mediation, but one of *direct correspondence*. The hypocrisy implicit in the separation of economic structure and cultural superstructure remains exactly the same if the economic process is made the determining cause, and it is left to mediation to give it a bashful covering with its dialectical veil. The only true materialism is one which radically abolishes this separation, never seeing in concrete historical reality the sum of structure and superstructure, but the direct unity of the two terms in praxis.

'The direct inference from the duty on wine to *L'Ame du vin*' is possible and necessary precisely because it is based on this correspondence. Perhaps then 'vulgar materialism', which directly relates structure and superstructure, is not vulgar at all, because in such directness a causal relationship cannot even be reasonably posited. Vulgarity is, rather, the attribute of that interpretation which, conceiving the relationship between structure and super-structure primarily as a relationship of cause and effect, needs 'mediation' and the 'total social process' to give a semblance of meaning to this relationship, and at the same time save its own idealist coyness.

To return to Adorno's 'magic' language, it could be said that dialectical historicism, whose spokesman he is, is the witch who, after turning the prince into a frog, believes she holds within the magic wand of dialectics the secret of any possible transformation. But historical materialism is the maiden who kisses the frog right on the mouth, and breaks the dialectical spell. For whereas the witch knows that, since every prince is really a frog, every frog can become a prince, the maiden does not know this, and her kiss touches precisely what the frog and the prince have in common.

In the light of these reflections, we must now consider Benjamin's method and his defence of it in his reply to Adorno. In accordance with an only apparently cryptographic purpose which characterizes Benjamin's intellectual stance, this defence takes the form of a crisis of philology in a perspective where the object of historical knowledge is presented as a 'monad'. The demand he places upon this formulation is that the materialist point of view within history cannot consist in writing (Marxist) history of art, (Marxist) history of philosophy, (Marxist) history of literature, etc., in which invariably structure and super-structure, perceived as distinct, are then theoretically connected in terms of the dialectics of the total social process; the only materialist point of view is that which radically overcomes the separation of structure and superstructure, because praxis is posited as the only single object in its original cohesion – that is, as 'monad' (the monad, according to Leibniz's definition, is a simple substance, 'without parts'). The task of guaranteeing the unity of this monad is entrusted to philology, whose object is in fact presented in a polar opposite of what, for Adorno, was a negative judgement: as an 'appearance of closed facticity' which excludes any ideological presupposition. Thus the monad of praxis is presented above all as a 'textual examination', as a hieroglyphic which the philologist must construct in its factitious integrity, in which elements of both structure and superstructure originally cohere in 'mythical rigidity'. Philology is the maiden who, without any dialectical precautions, kisses the frog of praxis on the mouth. What philology has thereby reaped in its closed facticity must, however, be construed in a historical perspective, by an operation which Benjamin defines as an *Aufhebung* of philology. The baselines of this perspective are not, however, to be found in the 'total social process' and 'good speculative theory', but 'in our own historical experience'. Only this has the potential to bring the object to life, detaching it from philology's mythical rigidity.

Benjamin illuminates this passage, in which philology and history find their most authentic connection, with a reference to his essay on 'Elective Affinities'.[7] It is worth quoting this passage at length, since it defines the relationship between the two fundamental concepts of 'subject matter' [*Sachgehalt*] and 'truth content' [*Wahrheitsgehalt*].

> Critique is concerned with the truth content of a work of art, the commentary with its subject matter. The relationship

between the two is determined by that basic law of literature according to which the work's truth content is the more relevant the more inconspicuously and intimately it is bound up with its subject matter. If therefore precisely those works turn out to endure whose truth is most deeply embedded in their subject matter, the beholder who contemplates them long after their own time finds the *realia* all the more striking in the work as they have faded away in the world. This means that subject matter and truth content, united in the work's early period, come apart during its afterlife; the subject matter becomes more striking while the truth content retains its original concealment. To an ever-increasing extent, therefore, the interpretation of the striking and the odd, that is, of the subject matter, becomes a prerequisite for any later critic. One may liken him to a paleographer in front of a parchment whose faded text is covered by the stronger outlines of a script referring to that text. Just as the paleographer would have to start with reading the script, the critic must start with commenting on his text. And out of this activity there arises immediately an inestimable criterion of critical judgment: only now can the critic ask the basic question of all criticism – namely, whether the work's shining truth content is due to its subject matter or whether the survival of the subject matter is due to the truth content. For as they come apart in the work, they decide on its immortality. In this sense the history of works of art prepares their critique, and this is why historical distance increases their power. If, to use a simile, one views the growing work as a funeral pyre, its commentator can be likened to the chemist, its critic to an alchemist. While the former is left with wood and ashes as the sole objects of his analysis, the latter is concerned only with the enigma of the flame itself: the enigma of being alive. Thus the critic inquires about the truth whose living flame goes on burning over the heavy logs of the past and the light ashes of life gone by.

The relationship delineated here between subject matter and truth content provides the model for what, in Benjamin's terms, could be the relationship between structure and superstructure. The historian who sees before him a divided structure and super-structure, and tries to give a dialectical explanation of the one as base for the other (either way, depending on whether he is an idealist or a materialist), can be likened to the chemist whom Benjamin describes, who sees only wood and ashes, while the historical materialist is the alchemist, his eyes fixed on the pyre, in which, like subject matter and truth content, structure and superstructure also become the same thing. And just as subject matter and truth content are originally unified in the work, and appear separate only within temporal duration, so structure and superstructure, unified in praxis, are separate in the work that survives through time. What looks upon us from the monuments and the rubble of the past and seems in them to refer, almost allegorically, to a hidden meaning, is not, then, a relic of the ideological superstructure, which, in order to be understood, has to be traced back, by a painstaking work of mediation, to the historical structure which determines it; quite the contrary – what we now have before us is praxis itself as origin and monadic historical structure. In becoming the nature of history, it splits (just as subject matter and truth content are separated in the work) and is enigmatically present as nature, as a petrified landscape which is to be brought back to life. The task of the critic is to recognize in the amazed facticity of the work, which is there as a philological exhibit, the direct and fundamental unity of subject matter and truth content, of structure and superstructure embedded in it.

The statement 'the structure is the superstructure' is not just a deterministic proposition in the causal sense; it is not even a dialectical proposition in the ordinary sense, where, in place of the predicate, should be set the slow process of negation and of the *Aufhebung*. It is a speculative proposition – that is to say, immobile and immediate. This is the meaning of the 'dialectic at a standstill' which Benjamin leaves as a legacy to historical materialism, and with which it must reckon sooner or later. For the time has come to end the identification of history with a conception of time as a continuous linear process, and to understand thereby that the dialectic is quite capable of being a historical category without, as a consequence, having to fall into linear time. It is not the dialectic which has to be adequate to a pre-existing, vulgar conception of time; on the contrary, it is this conception of time which must be adequate to a dialectic that is truly freed from all 'abstractness'.

NOTES

* In the *Studierzimmer* scene of Goethe's *Faust*, Part I, the student says: 'Was man schwarz auf weiss besitzt, kann man getrost nach Hause tragen.' (What one possesses in black and white one can safely take home.)

1. These letters, translated by Harry Zohn, appear in *Aesthetics and Politics*, London: Verso 1980, pp. 126–37.

2. In Walter Benjamin, *Charles Baudelaire – A Lyric Poet in the Era of High Capitalism*, transl. Harry Zohn, London: Verso 1983.

3. Theodor Adorno, 'A Portrait of Walter Benjamin', in *Prisms*, transl. Samuel and Shierry Weber, London: Neville Spearman 1967, p. 229.

4. ibid., p. 236.

5. G.W.F. Hegel, *Phenomenology of Spirit*, transl. A.V. Miller, Oxford: Clarendon Press 1977, p. 11.

6. Engels to J. Bloch, London to Königsberg, 21–22 September 1890, in *Marx-Engels Selected Works*, in one volume, London: Lawrence & Wishart 1968, p. 498.

7. This essay, 'Goethe's Elective Affinities', remains as yet untranslated in full. It first appeared in Hoffmannsthal's *Neue Deutsche Beiträge* (1924–5). The passage quoted here is translated in Hannah Arendt's Introduction to *Illuminations*, transl. Harry Zohn, Glasgow: Fontana 1973.

FABLE AND HISTORY

Considerations on the Nativity Crib

There is no way of understanding the crib if it is not first and foremost understood that the image of the world which it presents in miniature is a historical image. For what is shows us is the world of the fable precisely at the moment when it wakes from enchantment to enter history. The fable had been able to separate itself from initiation rites only by abolishing the experience of the mystery which was at its centre, and transforming it into enchantment. The creature of the fable is subjected to the trials of initiation and the silence of the mystery, but without experiencing them – in other words, by undergoing them as a spell. It is bewitchment rather than participation in secret knowledge that deprives it of speech; but this bewitchment is equally a disenchantment from the mystery and, as such, must be shattered and overcome. What became *fabula muta* (it is in this dense oxymoron that a character in Petronius' *Satyricon* crystallizes the mutism of the religions of late Antiquity, saying of Jove: '. . . inter coelicolas fabula muta taces') must rediscover the power of speech. Thus, in the fairy tale, while man, spellbound, is struck dumb, nature, spellbound, speaks. With this exchange of speech and silence, history and nature, the fairy tale prophesies its own disenchantment in history.

The crib grasps the world of the fairy tale in the messianic instant of this transition. Hence the animals who, in the fairy tale, left the pure, mute language of nature and spoke, are now dumbstruck. According to an ancient legend, for a moment on Christmas night animals acquire the power of speech: these are the creatures of fairy tales appearing for the last time in their enchantment before re-entering for ever the mute language of nature. In the words of the pseudonymous 'Matthews Bible',[1] to whom we owe the entry of the ox and ass into the iconography of the nativity: 'The ox knows its master and the ass the manger of the Lord'. In one of the earliest descriptions of the crib, Saint Ambrose counterposes the *whimpering* of the God-child, which is heard, with the silent *lowing* of the ox who recognizes his Lord. Objects, which enchantment had animated and made strange, are now returned to the innocence of the inorganic, and stand beside man as docile implements and familiar tools. Talking hens, ants and birds, the goose who lays the golden egg, the donkey who shits money, the table that sets itself and the stick that beats on command: the crib must release all this from its spell. As food, merchandise or instruments – in other words, in their humble economic apparel – nature and inorganic objects are bundled up on to the market stall, displayed on tables at inns (the inn – which, in fairy tale, is the site assigned for crime and deception – here recovers its reassuring garb) or hang from larder ceilings.

Man, too, whom the spell of the fairy tale had removed from his economic function, is now recognised to it with an exemplary gesture: the decisive gesture that severs the human world of the crib from that of the fairy tale. In the fairy tale, all is ambiguous gesticulation of law and magic, condemning or absolving, prohibiting or permitting, spellbinding or spellbreaking; or the enigmatic severity of astrological decans and figures, sanctioning the chain of destiny which binds all creatures (even if, on all this, the fairy tale unfurls the swooning veil of enchantment); while in the crib man is returned to the univocality and transparency of his historical gesture. Tailors and woodcutters, shepherds and peasants, greengrocers and butchers, hunters and innkeepers, roast-chestnut and water vendors: this whole profane universe of the market and the street emerges into history in a gesture from the prehistoric depths of that world which Bachofen defined as 'etheric', and which had a short-lived revival in Kafka's stories. It could be said that the somnolent and miasmic world of the fairy tale is the medium between the mysteries of the hierophants and the historical gesture of the crib.

For in the messianic night, the creature's gesture is loosed of any magical-juridical-divinatory density, and becomes simply human and profane. Here, there is no longer any sign or marvel in the divinatory sense; but, since all signs have their fulfilment, man is freed by signs: thus the sibyls in Alamanni's crib at San Giovanni in Carbonara stand mute before the manger, and in the Neapolitan cribs, the *térata* and the *monstra* of the classical reading of entrails appear as laughing grotesques (reminiscent of Giacomo Colombo's little figure of the goitred woman or the cripples by an anonymous eighteenth-century hand in the San Martino museum) which no longer signify some future event, merely the creature's profane innocence. Hence, in contrast to the static mystery of the early nativities, the realism with which the creatures are captured in their everyday gestures; hence, in a scene which should be the adoration of a god, the precocious absence of the iconographic convention of the adorer, so characteristic of scenes from pagan and palaeo-Christian cults. Only the representatives of the world of magic and law, the Magi, are featured in an act of adoration – at least to begin with, before they melt into the nameless crowd: elsewhere, all ritual traces dissolve into the economic innocence of the quotidian. Even the shepherds' offering of food has no sacrificial intention; it is a secular gesture rather than a ritual *piaculum*. The sleeper who, strangely, never fails to appear near the manger can perhaps be seen as a figure from the world of fairy tale, unable to wake on redemption and destined to continue his crepuscular life among children; even he does not sleep the sleep of the *incubatio*, laden with divinatory presages, nor, like the Sleeping Beauty, the timeless sleep of bewitchment, but the profane sleep of the living creature. As in the Book of James or *Protoevangelium* ('I Joseph was walking and I walked not . . . and they that were chewing chewed not. . . . And behold there were sheep being driven, and they went not forward but stood still; and the shepherd lifted his hand to smite them with his staff, and his hands remained up[2]) time stood still – not in the eternity of myth and fairy tale, but in the messianic interval between two moments, which is the time of history ('And of a sudden things moved onward in their course[3]). And at the beginning of the seventeenth century, when the first animated cribs will be constructed, the deeply allegorical intent of the Baroque will literally set the scansion of this historic 'walk without walking' in the rhymed repetition of the shepherd's step, or the movement of the grazing sheep.

The key to this profane liberation from enchantment is miniaturization, that 'salvation of the small' which – as is shown in every period by the taste for puppets, marionettes and those *bibelots* that eighteenth-century Europe called *petites besognes d'Italie* – is without doubt a defining feature of Italian cultural physiognomy, and which we can already see at work in the world of late Antiquity, almost like a counter-echo in which the rigidified world of the monumental entrusts its hope of historical awakening. Those same elements which Riegl so aptly discerned in miniatures, mosaics and late-Roman ivories – the axial isolation of the figures, the emancipation of space and the 'magical' linking of each thing – are found precisely in the crib. It is as if the 'miniaturist', the 'colourist' and the 'illusionist' (thus scholars christened the three unknown authors of the striking Genesis miniatures in Vienna, which are petrified in their mute astrological – fairy-tale *facies*) were miraculously guiding the hands of Celebrano, the Ingaldi, Giacomo Sanmartino, Lorenzo Mosca, Francesco Gallo, Tommaso Schettino and the anonymous figure-makers who still work in some surviving Neopolitan workshops. But the *magical* link between the figures has been completely resolved in a *historical* link. Each figure in the crib is certainly a whole in itself, not united with the others by any plastic or spatial tie, simply set momentarily beside them; however, all the figures, without exception, are welded into a single structure by the invisible adhesive of participation in the messianic event of the redemption. Even those cribs – like the Cuccitiello in the San Martino museum – in which the drive towards composition appears stronger are, in their intimate detail, a motley (for in essence they must have the potential to proliferate and expand to infinity); the ensemble's absolute unity is neither spatial nor material, but historical.

At the centre of the crib's figurative intent is not a mythic event or, even less, a spatio-temporal happening (that is, a chronological event), but a cairological event. It is in its essence a representation of the historicity which takes place in the world through the messianic birth. Thus in the sumptuous, endless proliferation of figures and episodes, in which the original sacred scene is well-nigh forgotten and the eye tires of searching for it, all distinctions between the sacred and the profane fall away, and the two spheres are bridged in history. Against the monumentality of a world now fixed and frozen in the inflexible laws of the *heimarméné* – laws not so dissimilar from the ones by which our own epoch feels itself, with jovial horror, being pushed and dragged into 'progress' – the crib counterpoises the minutiae of a history in what one might call its nascent state, in which everything is mere separate shred and splinter, but each sliver is immediately and historically complete.

This is why, at this very point when the crib is about to become an obsolete custom and seems even to have stopped speaking to the childhood which, as eternal guardian of what merits survival, had held it in safekeeping up to our time, together with play and fairy tale, the clumsy creatures of the last Neopolitan figurines seem to babble out a message intended for us, citizens of this extreme, threadbare fringe of a century of history. For the striking feature in the work of the anonymous survivors of Spaccanapoli is the infinite discrepancy between the figuring of man – whose lineaments are as if blurred in a dream, whose gestures are torpid and imprecise – and the delirious, loving impulse that shapes the displays of tomatoes, aubergines, cabbages, pumpkins, carrots, mullet, crayfish, octopus, mussels and lemons that lie in violet, red and iridescent mounds on the market stalls among baskets, scales, knives and earthenware pots. Are we to see, in this discrepancy, the sign that nature is once more about to enter the fairy tale, that once more it asks history for speech, while man – bewitched by a history which, for him, again assumes the dark outline of destiny – is struck dumb by a spell? Until one night, in the shadow-light where a new crib will light up figures and colours yet unknown, nature will once again be immured in its silent language, the fable will awaken in history, and man will emerge, with his lips unsealed, from mystery to speech.

NOTES

1. The 'Matthews Bible', issued in 1537 by John Rogers, under the pseudonym Thomas Matthews.
2. The Book of James, XVIII: 1, in *The Apocryphal New Testament*, transl. M.R. James, Oxford: Clarendon Press 1924, p. 46.
3. ibid.

NOTES ON GESTURE

I

By the end of the nineteenth century the gestures of the Western bourgeoisie were irretrievably lost.

In 1886 Gilles de la Tourette, formerly an intern at the Paris Hospital and the Salpêtrière, had his *Etudes cliniques et physiologiques sur la marche* published by Delahaye and Lecrosnier. Never before had one of the most common human gestures been analysed according to strictly scientific methods. Fifty-three years earlier, when the bourgeoisie was still untouched by scruples of conscience, the project of a general pathology of social life heralded by Balzac had produced naught but the fifty – when all was said and done, disappointing – pages of the *Théorie de la démarche*. Nothing discloses the distance – not only a temporal distance – which separates the two approaches as much as the description Gilles de la Tourette gives of a human step. Where Balzac saw only an expression of moral character, here the gaze at work is already prophetic of the cinema:

> With the leg as support, the right foot is raised from the ground in a rolling motion from the heel to the tips of the toes, which are the last part to be lifted away: the whole leg is brought forward, and the foot touches down at the heel. At this moment, the left foot, which has completed its roll and now rests only on the tips of the toes, in turn leaves the ground; the left leg is carried forward, moves closely alongside the right leg and goes past it, and the left foot touches the ground at the heel just as the right is finishing its roll forward.[1]

Only an eye endowed with a vision of this kind could formulate the footprint method which Gilles de la Tourette sets out so boldly to perfect. A roll of white wallpaper, around seven or eight metres long and fifty centimetres wide, is nailed to the floor and split in half lengthwise with a pencilled line. In the experiment the soles of the subject's feet are then sprinkled with powdered iron sesquioxide, which gives them a nice rust-red colour. The footprints left by the patient walking along the guiding line enable the gait to be measured with perfect precision according to different parameters (length of stride, distance breadthwise, angle of downward pressure, etc.).

If we study the reproductions of the footprints published by Gilles de la Tourette, we cannot fail to be reminded of the various series of split-second photographs that Eadweard Muybridge made in those very same years at the University of Pennsylvania, using a battery of twenty-four cameras. The 'man moving at a walking pace', the 'man running with a rifle', the 'woman walking and picking up a jug', the 'woman walking and blowing a kiss' are the visible and fortunate twins of those sick and anonymous creatures who have left these traces.

A year before the walking studies, Tourette had published his *Etude sur une affection nerveuse caractérisée par de l'incoordination motrice accompagnée d'écholalie et de coprolalie*, which was to provide the clinical context for what would later become known as Tourette's Syndrome. Here that same isolation of the most everyday movement that had been made possible by the footprint method is applied to a description of a staggering proliferation of tics, involuntary spasms and mannerisms that can be defined only as a generalized catastrophe of the gestural sphere. The patient is incapable of either beginning or fully enacting the most simple gestures; if he or she manages to initiate a movement, it is interrupted and sent awry by uncontrollable jerkings and shudderings whereby the muscles seem to dance (chorea) quite independently of any motor purpose. The equivalent of this disorder in the sphere of walking is described in exemplary manner by Charcot in the famous *Leçons du mardi*:

There he is, setting out with his body leaning forward, and the lower limbs rigid and held tight together balanced on tiptoe; they slide over the floor somehow, progressing by means of a kind of rapid twitching. . . when the subject has thrust himself forward in this way he appears at every moment to be on the verge of falling headlong; at any rate it is virtually impossible for him to stop of his own volition. Usually he needs to hang on to some other body near him. It's as if he's an automaton moved by a spring, and in these stiff forward movements, jerky like convulsions, there is nothing reminiscent of the looseness of walking. . . . In the end, after various attempts, he sets off, and following the mechanism just described, he slides rather than walks across the floor, with his legs stiff, or at least scarcely bending at all, with abrupt twitching movements somehow taking the place of steps.

What is most extraordinary is that after these disorders had been observed in thousands of cases from 1885 onwards, there is practically no further record of them in the early years of the twentieth century – until the winter's day in 1971 when Oliver Sacks, walking through the streets of New York, saw what he believed were three cases of Tourettism within the space of a few minutes. One of the hypotheses that can be constructed to explain this disappearance is that ataxy, tics and dystonia had, in the course of time, become the norm, and that beyond a certain point everyone had lost control of their gestures, walking and gesticulating frenetically. This, at least, is the impression one has in looking at the films that Marey and Lumière began to make in those very years.

II

In the cinema, a society that has lost its gestures seeks to re-appropriate what it has lost while simultaneously recording that loss.

An era that has lost its gestures is, for that very reason, obsessed with them; for people who are bereft of all that is natural to them, every gesture becomes a fate. And the more the ease of these gestures was lost under the influence of invisible powers, the more life became indecipherable. It is at this stage that the bourgeoisie – which, only a few decades earlier, had still been firmly in possession of its symbols – falls a victim to interiority and entrusts itself to psychology.

Nietzsche is the point where this polar tension in European culture reaches its peak – a tension towards the effacement and loss of the gesture on one hand and, on the other, its transmutation into a destiny. For it is only as a gesture in which potential and action, nature and artifice, contingency and necessity, become indiscernible (in the final analysis, therefore, solely as theatre) that the idea of eternal return makes sense. *Thus Spake Zarathustra* is the ballet of a humanity bereft of its gestures. And when the era became aware of this, then (too late!) began the headlong attempt to regain *in extremis* those lost gestures. The dance of Isadora and Diaghilev, the novels of Proust, the great *Jugendestil* poets from Pascoli to Rilke and ultimately – in the most exemplary way – silent cinema, trace the magic circle in which humanity sought, for the last time, to evoke what was slipping through its fingers for ever.

Contemporary with this, Aby Warburg was initiating those researches which only the short-sightedness of a psychologizing art history could describe as 'a science of the image', whereas in reality, at their centre was gesture as a crystal of historical memory, its hardening into a fate, and the strenuous effort of artists and philosophers (verging on madness in Warburg's case) to free it from this by means of a polarizing dynamic. Because these researches were conducted by means of images, it was believed that the image was also their object. Instead, Warburg transformed the image (which for Jung will furnish the model of the metahistoric sphere of archetypes) into a resolutely historical and dynamic element. In this sense, the *Mnemosyne* atlas, with its two thousand or so photographs, which he left unfinished, is not a fixed repertoire of images, but virtually a moving representation of the gestures of Western humankind from classical Greece up to Fascism (in other words, something closer to De Jorio than to Panovsky). Within each section the individual images are treated more as the frames of a film than as an autonomous reality (at least in the sense intended by Benjamin when he compared the dialectical image with those little picture-books prefiguring the cinema, which, when their pages are turned quickly, give the impression of motion).

III

Gesture rather than image is the cinematic element.

Gilles Deleuze has shown that cinema wipes out the fallacious psychological distinction between image as psychic reality and movement as physical reality. Film images are neither 'timeless postures' (like the forms of the classical world) nor 'static sections' of movement, but 'moving sections', images which are themselves in motion, which Deleuze calls 'moving-pictures'. We need to extend Deleuze's analysis and show that it has a general bearing on the status of the image within modernity. But this means that the mythical fixity of the image has been broken, and we should not really speak of images here, but of gestures. In fact, every image is animated by an antinomous polarity: on the one hand this is the reification and effacement of a gesture (the *imago* either as symbol or as the wax mask of the corpse); on the other it maintains the *dynamis* (as in Muybridge's split-second photographs, or in any photograph of a sporting event). The former corresponds to the memory of whose voluntary recall it takes possession; the latter to the image flashed in the epiphany of involuntary memory. And while the former dwells in magical isolation, the latter always refers beyond itself, towards a whole of which it is a part. Even the *Mona Lisa*, even Velázquez's *Meninas*, can be seen not as timeless static forms but as fragments of a gesture or as frames of a lost film, solely within which would they regain their true meaning. For in every image there is always a kind of *ligatio* at work, a power that paralyses, whose spell needs to be broken; it is as if, from the whole history of art, a mute invocation were raised towards the freeing of the image in the gesture. This much was expressed in those Greek legends about statues breaking the fetters that contain them and beginning to move; but it is also the intention that philosophy entrusts to the idea, which is not at all – as it is commonly interpreted – a static archetype, but rather a constellation in which phenomena are composed in a gesture.

Cinema leads images back into the realm of gesture. According to the splendid definition implicit in Beckett's *Traum und Nacht*, this is the dream of a gesture. Bringing the element of awakening into this dream is the task of the film-maker.

IV

Because it is centrally located in the gesture, not the image, cinema essentially ranks with ethics and politics (and not merely with aesthetics).

What is gesture? An observation by Varro holds an extremely valuable clue. He inscribes gesture in the sphere of action, but distinguishes it clearly from acting [*agere*] and doing [*facere*]:

A person can make [*facere*] something and not enact [*agere*] it, as a poet makes a play, but does not act it (*agree* in the sense of playing a part); on the other hand the actor acts the play, but does not make it. So the play is made [*fit*] by the poet, but not acted [*agitur*] by him; it is acted by the actor, but not made by him. Whereas the *imperator* (the magistrate in whom supreme power is invested) of whom the expression *res gerere* is used (to carry something out, in the sense of taking it upon oneself, assuming total responsibility for it), neither makes nor acts, but takes charge, in other words carries the burden of it [*sustinet*].[2]

What characterizes gesture is that in it there is neither production nor enactment, but undertaking and supporting. In other words, gesture opens the sphere of *ethos* as the most fitting sphere of the human. But in what way is an action undertaken and supported? In what way does a *res* become *res gesta*, a simple fact become an event? Varro's distinction between *facere* and *agere* derives, in the final analysis, from Aristotle. In a famous passage from the *Nicomachean Ethics*, he contrasts them thus: 'Action [*praxis*] and production [*poiesis*] are generically different. For production aims at an end other than itself; but this is impossible in the case of action, because the end is merely to do what is right.'

What is new, however, is the identification, along with these, of a third kind of action: if doing is a means in sight of an end and praxis is an end without means, gesture breaks the false alternative between ends and means that paralyses morality and presents means which, *as such*, are removed from the sphere of mediation without thereby becoming ends.

Thus, if we are to understand gesture, nothing is more misleading than to picture a sphere of means directed towards an end (for example, walking as a means of moving the body from point A to point B) and hence, distinct from and superior to it, a sphere of gesture as movement that contains its own end within itself (for example, dance as an aesthetic dimension). A finality without means is just as much of an aberration as a mediation that makes sense only in relation to an end. If dance is gesture, this is, however, because it is nothing but the physical tolerance of bodily movements and the display of their mediating nature. *Gesture is the display of mediation, the making visible of a means as such.* It makes apparent the human state of being-in-a-medium and thereby opens up the ethical dimension for human beings. But as a person in a pornographic film is captured in the act of carrying out a gesture that is merely a means directed towards the end of procuring pleasure for others (or for him or herself), through the sole fact of being photographed and displayed in his or her own state of mediation this person is suspended from that mediation and can become, for the spectators, the medium of a new pleasure (one that would be otherwise incomprehensible); or as those gestures in mime directed towards the most familiar ends are displayed as such, and therefore, held in suspense 'entre le désir et l'accomplissement, la perpétration et son souvenir'[3], in what Mallarmé calls a *milieu pur* – a pure milieu – thus, in gesture, there is the sphere not of an end in itself, but of a kind of mediation that is pure and devoid of any end that is effectively communicated to people.

Only in this way can the obscure Kantian expression 'finality without end' acquire a concrete meaning. It is, in a means, that potential for the gesture to interrupt it in its very being-means and only thus does it display it, does it turn a *res* into a *res gesta*. In the same way, if by word we intimate the means of communication, showing a word does not mean deploying something on a higher plane (a metalanguage which is itself incommunicable within the first level), on the basis of which this would be made an object of communication, but exposing it without any transcendence in its own state of mediation, in its own being as a means. In this sense, gesture is the communication of a potential to be communicated. In itself it has nothing to say, because what it shows is the being-in-language of human beings as a pure potential for mediation. But since being-in-language is not something that can be spoken of in propositions, in its essence gesture is always a gesture of a non-making of sense in language, it is always a gag in the strict meaning of the term, indicating in the first instance something that is put in the mouth to hinder speech, and subsequently the actor's improvisation to make up for a memory lapse or some impossibility of speech. Hence there is not only a proximity between gesture and philosophy, but also one between philosophy and cinema. The essential 'mutism' of cinema (which has nothing to do with either the presence or absence of a sound track) is, like the mutism of philosophy, an exposition of the human being's being-in-language: pure gesturality. The Wittgensteinian definition of mysticism as the showing of what cannot be spoken of, is a literal definition of the gag. And every great philosophical text is the gag that displays language itself, being-in-language itself, as a giant memory lapse, as an incurable speech defect.

V

Politics is the sphere of pure means, which is to say of the absolute and total gesturality of human beings.

NOTES

1. 'La jambe servant de point d'appui, le pied droit se soulève du sol en subissant un mouvement d'enroulement allant du talon à l'extremité des orteils qui quittent terre en dernier lieu: la jambe toute entière est portée en avant, passe à côté de la jambe droite dont elle tend à se rapprocher, la dépasse et le pied gauche vient toucher le sol par le talon alors que le droit achève sa révolution.'
2. Varro, *De Lingua Latina*, VI, 77.
3. 'between the desire and its fulfilment, the perpetration and its memory'. (Trans.)

PROJECT FOR A REVIEW

The review whose project is presented here makes its claims to authority in precise proportion to its awareness of its own situation. Only in so far as it attains such awareness – at a time that has lost sight of any other criterion for events than 'what the newspapers say', just when 'what the newspapers say' no longer has a jot to do with reality – can it aspire without arrogance to find within itself the criterion of its own timeliness. The point of view which it intends to adopt is in fact so radically and originally historical that it can easily renounce any chronological perspective, instead including among its tasks a 'destruction' of literary historiography. The site it chooses to inhabit is neither a continuity nor a new beginning, but an interruption and a margin, and it is the experience of this margin as founding historical event which constitutes the very basis of its timeliness.

The margin in question is the one produced early in modern Western culture between cultural patrimony and its transmission, between truth and its modes of transmission, between writing and authority. Our culture is such a long way from having noticed this margin that even its formulation without recourse to categories borrowed from other cultures presents almost insurmountable difficulties. For a more precise perception of it one could use the Talmudic categories of *Halacha* (the Law in itself, the truth separated from any mythical consistency) and *Aggada* (the Law in its emotional consistency, in its translatability), or the Arabic categories of *sharī' at* and *haqīqat*, which designate the Law in its literalness and its spiritual sense, respectively; or have recourse to the two categories 'subject matter' and 'truth content', whose primary unity and separation in the course of time, in Benjamin's view, mark the essence and historicity of the work of art.

In these terms, Western culture could be characterized as being irreparably driven between *Halacha* and *Aggada*, between *sharī' at* and *haqīqat*, between subject matter and truth content. Any healing between these terms has become impossible (this, incidentally, is evident in the loss of the commentary and the gloss as creative forms) – at least ever since the demise of the medieval theory of the four meanings of writing. (This theory has nothing to do with the gratuitous exercise of four successive and distinct interpretations of a text; rather, it takes its place among them, in the living relationship between subject matter and truth content.) Thus there is a truth, without the possibility of transmitting it; there are modes of transmission, without anything being either transmitted or taught.

This is the essential disjunction that recurs time and again in our culture as contrast between old and new, past and present, *anciens* and *modernes*. What this *querelle* now prevents us from seeing is that old and new alike have become obdurately inaccessible. For it is untrue that our time can be characterized merely by its obliviousness to traditional values and a scepticism about the past. On the contrary, perhaps no other epoch has been so obsessed by its own past and so unable to create a vital relationship with it, so mindful of *Halacha* and so unfit to give it an aggadic consistency. In our century estrangement and the ready-made, appropriation and quotation, have represented the last attempts to reconstruct this relationship (at its moments of commitment, the avant-garde has never turned to the future, but represents an extreme effort to relate to the past). Their decline marks the start of a time in which the present, petrified in an archaic *facies*, remains always a wasteland, while the past, in its estranged mask of modernity, can be only a monument to the present.

It is this cleavage, this margin, which the review claims as its site. For if the phenomenon we have described certainly concerns

Western culture as a whole, it is nevertheless in Italian culture that it is most prevalent. By comparison with other European cultures, Italian culture is a specific case, in that there is not merely a rigidified tradition which must be restored to its original fluidity, but from the start the cultural heritage was never yoked to its transmission; the *Halacha* did not find its own *Aggada*. The margin where the review will place itself, therefore, is the original event, which, for Italian culture, has not yet ceased to take place. Nothing here has reached its end, because nothing has yet begun: there is no beginning because everything starts from the end. As a result, in this culture all traditions are false, all authorities are convinced by lies; but, just as directly, all appeals to the new fall back into the past, all demystifications are mystifications. Hence the particular fragility of all intellectual positions in Italy, which invariably seem in perpetual dread of being swept away. Hence too the strength of those who realize that there is no living tradition to bestow legitimacy; they are relics already, already swept away, but as relics they do not fear the gusts of wind, and can even send out signals.

The task imposed on the review by its situation cannot thereby simply be defined as a 'destruction', albeit a necessary one, of tradition, but rather as a 'destruction of destruction', in which the destruction of the mode of transmission, which marks our culture fundamentally, is dialectically brought to light. It is only in a 'destruction' of this kind that the categorical structures of Italian culture can become visible, like the architectural skeleton of a house in flames. The choice of comedy and the refusal of tragedy; the domination of the architectural element and a sensibility so defenceless in the face of beauty that it can grasp it only nebulously; the pre-eminence of the Law together with a theological conception of human innocence; a primitive interest in the fairy tale as an enchanted world of guilt, and its Christian redemption in the 'historical' miniature of the Nativity crib; an interest in historiography alongside a conception of human life as 'fable' – these are some of the categories on whose antinomic tension the Italian phenomenon rests.

Thus philology, beyond the limits of any narrow academic conception, will occupy a particular place in this review. Indeed, this philology must serve as the tool of its 'destruction of destruction'. In our culture, which lacks specific categories for spiritual transmission and exegesis, it has always fallen to philology to guarantee the authenticity and continuity of the cultural tradition. This is why a knowledge of philology's essence and history should be a precondition of all literary education; yet this very knowledge is hard to find even among philologists. Instead, as far as philology is concerned, confusion and indifference reign. Thus the literary and artistic avant-gardes, which are undoubtedly a form of philology – as even a superficial analysis of their methods could easily prove – are placed within the history of art and literature, while to the human and philological sciences are ascribed studies which are undoubtedly poetic works. And it remains to be adequately investigated why it was Western culture that produced philology as a rigorous science; and why, at every renewal of this science, it was poets (Philetas and Callimachus in the Hellenic period, Petrarch and Poliziano during early Humanism, and Friedrich Schlegel in the Romantic period) who were impelled to become philologists. By not confining itself to the material transmission of texts, but claiming as specific tasks the *emendatio* and the *coniectura* (correction and conjecture), philology reveals its specific place between *Halacha* and *Aggada*, between truth and transmission, between subject matter and truth content. Examples of illustrious philologists who were falsifiers – usually covered up, with an embarrassed silence, as aberrant phenomena – betray the singular claim which distinguishes the essence of philology.

The abolition of the margin between the thing to be transmitted and the act of transmission, and between writing and authority, has in fact been philology's role since the very beginning. And since this abolition has always been regarded as the essential character of myth, philology can thereby be defined as a 'critical mythology'. The 'new mythology' – to which Schelling assigned the role of mediating the reuniting of poetry and science in our time, and about which he asked: 'How could a mythology be born that was not the invention of a single poet, but of a generation?' There already exists the new poetry that the modern poets – from Blake to Rilke, from Novalis to Yeats – vainly tried to create, and it is a philology aware of its task (philology here stands for all the critical-philological disciplines which today are designated, somewhat inappropriately, 'human sciences').

Both the 'wide-eyed presentation of mere facts' and the magical devotion to detail, which Benjamin recognized as characterizing the true philological attitude; and the definition of philology as *philomythos* and *fabellae studiosus* which is encountered in Poliziano's *Lamia*, that manifesto of modern philology, bear witness to this kinship between critical-philological disciplines and mythology which must be elucidated anew. Essentially and historically, philology is an *Aufhebung* of mythology; it is always a *fabulari ex re*. But the 'mythical rigidity' of philology's material must be animated by criticism, and its object must be constructed within a perspective whose baselines converge on our own historical experience. It is this *Aufhebung* of philology which the review proposes to bring about, taking a stance where, as 'critical mythology', it has an exact correspondence with poetry. In accordance with Vico's definition, which numbers 'poets, historians, orators, grammarians' among philologists, one of the review's founding principles will be to place critical philological disciplines on precisely the same plane as poetry. Poetry and philology: poetry as philology and philology as poetry. Of course it is not a matter of inviting poets to produce works of philology and philologists to write poetry, but both groups should occupy a site where the fracturing of the word which divides poetry and philosophy in Western culture becomes a conscious, problematic experience rather than an embarrassed repression. We have in mind not only authors such as Benjamin or Poliziano, Callimachus or Valéry – who are so difficult to classify in any precise category – but also those poets – like Dante and the author of the *Zohar*, Hölderlin and Kafka – who, in culturally diverse situations, made of the margin between truth and its transmission their central experience. And in the same terms, special attention must be reserved for translation, a critical-poetic act *par excellence*.

Thus can take shape and substance the project of an 'inter-disciplinary discipline' in which all the human sciences converge, together with poetry, and whose goal would be that 'general science of the human' which is severally heralded as the cultural task of the coming generation. In so far as it is possible, the review sets out to prepare the advent of this as yet unnamed science which, in its correspondence with poetry, might also be the new, critical mythology as described above (critical in the sense of freed from subjection to the powers of Law and Destiny, and restored to history).

It is implicit in an undertaking of this kind that the review must restore to criticism its status and its violence. It is the privilege of this status and this violence that it is not required to lay bare its own connection with politics. The original cohesion of poetry and politics in our culture was sanctioned from the very start by the fact that Aristotle's treatment of music is contained in the *Politics*, and that Plato's themes of poetry and art are to be found in the *Republic*; it is therefore a matter beyond dispute. The question is not so much whether poetry has any bearing on politics, but whether politics remains equal to its original cohesion with poetry. If criticism wishes to restore politics to its true dimension, it must first and foremost situate itself in antithesis to ideology, which has usurped this cohesion through its dissolution. 'False conscious-ness', whose dark clarity everywhere impedes access to the pro-blems of our time, must be hurled into the very abyss whose gaping width it seeks to preserve. Also implicit in the philological project of the review is a revision of the concept of history which has dominated modern historicism. The moment has come to end the identification of history with a vulgar concept of time as a continuous linear and infinite process, and thereby to take cognizance of the fact that historical categories and temporal categories are not necessarily the same thing. It is a precondition of the review's proposed undertaking to reach a new point in the relationship between time and history – that is, first and foremost, a new and more primary experience of time and history. There must be a critical demolition of the ideas of process, development, and progress whereby historicism seeks to reinsert the pseudo-meanings of the Christian 'history of salvation' into a history which it has itself reduced to a pure chronology. Against the empty, continuous, quantified, infinite time of vulgar historicism must be set the full, broken, indivisible and perfect time of concrete human experience; instead of the chronological time of pseudo-history, the cairological time of authentic history; in place of the total social process of a dialectic lost in time, the interruption and immediacy of dialectic at a standstill. The critique of historical reason undertaken by Dilthey in the terms of a critical foundation for the human sciences must be brought to fruition – not in order to abandon history, but in order to attain a more original concept of it. Count Yorck's statement: 'Modern man, that is, post-Renaissance man, is ready for burial' must be integrated with Valéry's: 'The age of the world's end is beginning'. Thus the *Aufhebung* of philology moves through a new experience of history, and the site occupied by the review is at one with its method.

HISTORICO-PHILOLOGICAL NOTATION

It is not in historiography but in philology that we must seek the model for a concept of history which, by its independence from chronology, can simultaneously free myth from its archetypal isolation.

What is an Indo-European form (for example, *deiwos*, *ar-*, *wegh*, *med*) restored through philological comparison of the respective forms of the historical languages? What is a state of the language historically unattested and restored in this way through comparison? What is thus verified is undoubtedly, as with myth, a production of origins, but these origins are not an archetypal event separated in *illo tempore*, but are themselves essentially historical. Their 'historicity' cannot, however, be construed in an exclusively diachronic sense, as if it were merely a matter of a chronologically earlier stage of the language: as 'a defined system of correspondences' it represents, instead, a present and operative tendency in the historical languages. It is an origin, but an origin that is not diachronically pushed back into the past; rather, it guarantees the synchronic coherence of the system. In other words, it expresses something which cannot conveniently be described either in purely diachronic terms or in exclusively synchronic terms, but can be conceived only as a margin and a difference between diachrony and synchrony. We can define this margin as a historical *arkhē*, to distinguish it from a precise and continuous instant of traditional chronology. The legitimacy of a 'synchronic historicity' of this kind is scientifically based – at least from the starting point of Jakobson's *Principles of Historical Phonology*, which introduced historicity and teleology into categories supremely regarded as static and synchronic, opening the way to a consideration of language that allows mediation between descriptive linguistics and historical linguistics. From this point of view the opposition of structures and history is revealed to be inadequate; as *arkhai*, the Indo-European forms are not strictly either structural or historical, either synchronic or diachronic.

Arguing against structuralist theses, Dumézil characterized the object of his own comparative mythology: 'My efforts are not those of a philosopher, they aim to be those of a historian: a historian of the earliest history and the fringe of ultra-history that can reasonably be reached.' But what is this 'fringe of ultra-history' but an *arkhē* in the above sense? Because it can certainly never be resolved wholly into events which can be supposed to have taken place chronologically, unless the intention is to legitimate the *monstrum* of historiographical research producing its own original documents. What is described here as ultra-history is something that has not yet ceased to take place and which, exactly like the system of myth, guarantees the intelligibility of history and its synchronic coherence. From this point of view, Indo-European 'words' are equivalent to mythic names: not causes, but origins.

This is the sense in which philology can be called a 'critical mythology'. For it is philology – albeit standing in the way of myth – which can allow us to reconstruct an authentic, therefore free, relationship with it. For philology awakens myth from its arche-typal rigidity and its isolation, returning it to history. Its work of criticism produces an origin freed from any ritual character and any subjection to destiny. Its relationship to myth recalls child-hood's relationship to the mythic past of humanity. Just as children, in games and fairy tales, preserve the world of myth freed from its subjection to ritual, transforming the divinatory practice into the game of chance, the soothsayer's rod into the spinning top, the fertility rite into the circle game, so philology transforms mythic names into words, simultaneously delivering history from chronology and mechanism. What delineated the tight linguistic chain of destiny here becomes the linguistic substance of history. Critical mythology is the legacy left by philology, in the form of a vocabulary of Indo-European words, like a new infancy for Western culture. It must now pass into the hands of poetry.